AF556282

PRAISE FOR IN AND OUT OF CRISIS

Once again, Panitch, Gindin, and Albo show that they have few rivals and no betters in analyzing the relations between politics and economics, between globalization and American power, between theory and quotidian reality, and between crisis and political possibility. At once sobering and inspiring, this is one of the few pieces of writing that I've seen that's essential to understanding—to paraphrase a term from accounting—the sources and uses of crisis. Splendid and essential.

Doug Henwood, *Left Business Observer*, author of *After the New Economy* and *Wall Street*

In and Out of Crisis is a salutary reminder that knee-jerk reactions to current events are not the best way forward for the Left. What we need is careful investigation combined with practical experiences on campaigns to develop our movement. This book not only gives us a course in the global financial meltdown, but it also provides a model for how the Left must develop its alternatives, not *ex nihilo*, but from a study of the contradictions of the present.

Vijay Prashad, author of *Darker Nations: A People's History of the Third World*

A magnificent book. Seldom has political economy been done so thoroughly, and presented with such flair and authority. The authors' searching and open-minded scrutiny overturns most conventional thinking about the capitalist crisis and its alternatives.

Andrej Grubacic, radical historian, sociologist, and co-author of *Wobblies and Zapatistas*

Mired in political despair? Planning your escape to a more humane continent? Baffled by the economy? Convinced that the Left is out of ideas? Pull yourself together and read this book, in which Albo, Gindin, and Panitch, some of the world's sharpest living political economists, explain the current financial crisis—and how we might begin to make a better world.

Liza Featherstone, author of *Students Against Sweatshops* and *Selling Women Short: The Landmark Battle for Worker's Rights at Wal-Mart*

In and Out of Crisis, by three leading North American socialists, could not come at a more important time. The crisis of neoliberal globalization compels the Left to better understand the dynamics of global capitalism, the U.S. empire, but also the tasks confronting us. Albo, Gindin, and Panitch do not offer a blueprint, but instead provide us with a framework in order to develop a strategy for a renewed Left. This book pushes the envelope and bravo for that!

Bill Fletcher, Jr., Executive Editor, BlackCommentator.com, co-author of *Solidarity Divided*

In and Out of Crisis is a major contribution to a Left struggling to find its way. Offering a sharp analysis of capitalist crisis that recognizes the importance of struggles in the community and at the workplace, this book should be right next to leaflets, chant sheets, and protest signs in the backpacks of every organizer and activist looking to turn crisis into opportunity, and austerity into liberation.

Steve Williams, co-director and co-founder, People Organized to Win Employment Rights (POWER)

In and Out of the Crisis is a timely primer on the political economy of the present. It paints a clear picture of the financial crisis and the parlous state of unions and the working class, while offering little solace for those who think Obama liberalism is going to set things right. Rather, the authors call for a Left with the imagination to make big demands, such as universal health care, industrial planning, and bank nationalization. Even more, they call for a renewed faith in popular democracy in place of the smothering embrace of capital and the imperial state. This is essential reading for every student activist, political blogger, and labor militant in North America.
Richard Walker, Geography, University of California, Berkeley, and author of *The Capitalist Imperative*, *The New Social Economy*, *The Conquest of Bread* and *The Country in the City*.

This trio offers the Left a refreshing analysis of how we arrived in the Great Recession as well as a possible way out of capitalism as we know it.
Pratap Chatterjee, author of *Halliburton's Army* and *Iraq, Inc.*

The best analysis of our current moment in the U.S. has been written by Canadians!
Elizabeth Oram, activist and nurse

Greg Albo, Sam Gindin, and Leo Panitch provide a perceptive, and persuasive, analysis of the dominance of the corporate financial sector, overseen and managed by the U.S. state. They make a compelling argument that the Left must go beyond the demand for re-regulation, which, they argue, will not solve the economic or environmental crisis, and must instead demand public control of the banks and the financial sector, and of the uses to which finance is put. The linked economic and environmental crises, they argue, cannot be resolved as long as the logic of the market holds sway; the Left must demand that it be replaced by collective planning based on social and environmental needs. This is an important book that should be read widely, especially by those hoping to revitalize the Left.
Barbara Epstein, History of Consciousness, University of California, Santa Cruz, author of *The Minsk Ghetto* and *Political Protest and Cultural Revolution*

A penetrating examination of the current crisis and the state of capital, most interestingly in that it brings to the center of its analysis the condition of the working classes, arguing that as a result of a disorganized left and a marginalized workers' movement, the crisis in fact favors the capitalist classes. This in turn is a result of three decades of labor retreat and defeat and an inheritance of the worst in business unionism. Albo, Gindin and Panitch propose a formidable array of alternative tactics, strategies and principles.
Cal Winslow, author of *Labor's Civil War in California* and co-author, with Aaron and Robert Brenner, of *Rebel Rank and File: Labor Militancy and Revolt from Below During the Long 1970s*

IN AND OUT OF CRISIS

The Global Financial Meltdown and Left Alternatives

Greg Albo
Sam Gindin
Leo Panitch

IN AND OUT OF CRISIS
Greg Albo, Sam Gindin and Leo Panitch

Published in agreement with PM Press, Oakland, CA for publication and sale only in the Indian Subcontinent (India, Pakistan, Bangladesh, Nepal, Maldives, Bhutan & Sri Lanka)

First Published in India, 2011

ISBN 978-93-5002-054-8 (Hb)

Published by
AAKAR BOOKS
28 E Pocket IV, Mayur Vihar Phase I, Delhi 110 091
Phone : 011 2279 5505 Telefax : 011 2279 5641
aakarbooks@gmail.com; www.aakarbooks.com

Printed at
Mudrak, 30 A, Patparganj, Delhi 110 091

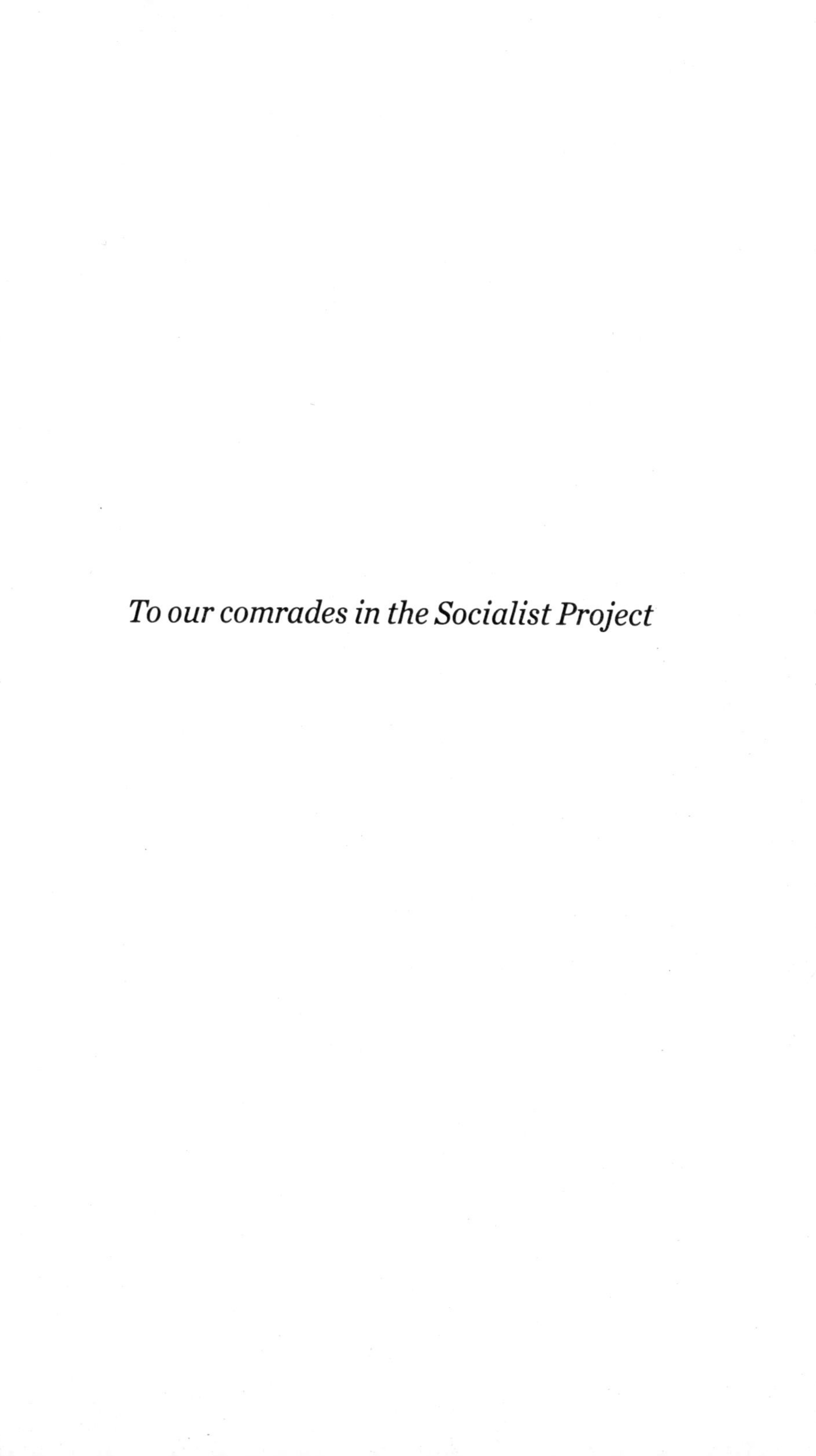

To our comrades in the Socialist Project

CONTENTS

PREFACE

"Capitalism Is Crisis," "Capitalism Is Not Working," "Their Crisis, Not Ours": banners like these have frequently popped up at demonstrations over the last three years. There can be little doubt that the financial crisis that exploded in the summer of 2007 in the U.S. subprime mortgage market had immense political as well as economic implications. For the first time since the presidency of Ronald Reagan in the early 1980s, the neoliberal counter-revolution he helped launch seemed to be succumbing to the accumulating contradictions in financial markets, growing social inequalities and faltering U.S. power in the world order. It has been some time since the slogans and analysis of the North American Left have held such popular resonance.

The classical meaning of crisis is turning point. The economic turbulence and social hardships that crises bring with them are in evidence everywhere one looks, with a decade of economic restructuring and austerity being suggested by the powers that be. But apart from undermining the mythology of self-regulating markets that has been so integral to the ideology of neoliberalism, has this crisis actually marked a turning point in the balance of class power and the organization of the state? Or can the political alliances and power structures that have dominated the last decades be re-assembled in what so clearly has been a monumental crisis of their own making? Crises pose these kinds of sharp political questions, and that is precisely why they are defining historical moments. The key to understanding crises as they are played out in history does not lie in the amount of capital destroyed in a recession, or in the volume of credit created as capital accumulation sputters and then re-starts, or in this or that policy innovation, but in the class politics and struggles that block, permit and execute various strategies to advance material interests. This book will investigate some of these class strategies in the making of the financial crisis and in shaping the struggles out of the crisis.

In doing so, this book departs from the common tendency on the Left no less than on the Right to judge economic and political developments through the prism of states versus markets, with each crisis marking an oscillation between one pole and the other. There are many conceptual and political traps in such a binary opposition. On the one hand, it suggests that markets can be potentially self-sufficient and that somehow states—as the underwriters of a vast administrative and physical infrastructure necessary for markets to exist at all and as guarantors of private property—can be marginalized. On the other, it proposes that the state can compensate for market failures and act as a neutral policy mechanism to offset private interests by governing in the public interest. Both miss the point that capitalist markets and capitalist states are deeply intertwined in the class and power structures of global capitalism. This book explores, in particular, the extent of the American state's entanglement in financial markets.

This is a historic moment when the ruling elites—from the financiers through the Detroit auto executives to liberal politicians—have lost credibility. Yet labor and the Left are still on the defensive. Being realistic today means daring to put forward something really new on the political agenda. Rather than perpetuating dependence on markets, competition, private corporations, and the values and pressures they represent, the Left needs to be organizing around an independent vision. The alternatives needed are not technical solutions to capitalist economic crises, but political ones that challenge property rights in the name of democratic and social rights. This involves a transformation in Left culture, one which can't really begin, let alone succeed unless it is part of the widest degree of discussion and debate about economic and political possibilities; mobilizes within and across the gender, racial and ethnic diversities of working class communities;

and develops strategies for identifying allies and building new popular, union and community capacities. This book seeks to make a contribution to this.

As is the case with all such contributions, this book is a product of collective efforts. It was Sasha Lilley who originally suggested we put this book together and her outstanding editing work greatly improved it. The book is also in many ways the product of the intensive discussions we have had with our former and current graduate students in the political science department at York University; we are especially grateful to Martijn Konings and Scott Aquanno for their contribution to our analysis of the subprime crisis. The ideas here have also been aired and developed at events sponsored by the *Socialist Register* and the Rosa Luxemburg Stiftung, especially at Historical Materialism and Left Forum conferences. We especially want to convey our appreciation to Pance Stojkovski for his creative work on *The Bullet*, the e-bulletin of the Socialist Project, where parts of the text presented here first appeared. It is to our comrades in the Socialist Project, our political home in Canada, that this book is dedicated.

Greg Albo, Sam Gindin, Leo Panitch
Toronto, January 2010

CHAPTER ONE

SURVEYING THE CRISIS: IS NEOLIBERALISM OVER?

Even the briefest of tallies of the economic crisis causes one to stare in disbelief at the casualties as the wreckage is registered. It amounted to the worst recession in the core advanced capitalist countries since the Great Depression, involving an overall decline in world output, with over 15 million people—or 10 percent of the labor force—officially unemployed in the United States at the beginning of 2010. Following 1.3 million home foreclosures in 2007 in the U.S., there were 2.3 million more in 2008, and the numbers continued to rise all the way through to 2010. Apart from the massive bailouts of the banks, the crisis was punctuated by the collapse the $65 billion Ponzi scheme, the largest in history, run by Bernard L. Madoff, the former head of the NASDAQ stock exchange; the takeover by the U.S. government of AIG, the biggest insurance company in the world; and the largest filing ever for Chapter 11 bankruptcy protection by General Motors in the summer of 2009. The Obama Administration's $787 billion emergency economic stabilization package was the most colossal stimulus measure in history. The U.S. budget deficit that same year, at over 12 percent of GDP, was not only the highest since World War II, but is expected to remain at this historic level for years to come.

Given how central the American economy is to global capitalism, the financial crisis that erupted in the U.S. housing market in 2007 spread around the world with lightning speed. The ensuing "Great Recession" sent one economy after another crashing down. The satirical broadsheet *The Onion* captured this perverse example of the imperial relationship between the U.S. and the rest of the world with a headline in November 2007: "Bush Proud the U.S. Can Cause Markets around the World to Collapse." Even the surging economies of East Asia, notably China, could not escape the economic storm brewed in the U.S. financial system. The depth and global scope of the downturn left states with little choice initially but to introduce massive public expenditures, not only to save the banks but to try to stimulate the economy. Working families, experiencing the frightening erosion of their effective savings—their pensions and home values—cut back on consumption in order to rebuild some future security. Private investors, seeing few opportunities and reacting with caution and uncertainty toward the future, were no longer investing in anything except safe government bonds.

At least in the so-called efficient markets theory guiding financial regulators, none of this was supposed to occur. Three decades of policies oriented to enhancing markets, freer trade, and "disciplining" workers and unions was meant not only to bring prosperity to all, but also greater economic stability. Each of the financial panics—the Savings and Loans crisis of the 1980s, the Long Term Capital Management and Asian financial crisis of the late 1990s, the dot-com meltdown—that have paralleled the evolution of these policies were always considered exceptional events and unlikely to be repeated. But none of these raised the levels of fears and doubts about the merits of capitalism from within the citadels of global finance.

In the midst of the banking turmoil of 2008, Wall Street mavens expressed alarm that the "best of all possible worlds" for financiers had suddenly gone deeply wrong. Leading bankers at Morgan Stanley, Goldman Sachs and others began to openly worry that a second Great Depression loomed. The *Financial Times*, now the paper of record for financial and political elites across the globe, took the doubts to the point of running a series of essays on the future of capitalism. The articles concluded, not surprisingly, that capitalism does indeed have a future. But they questioned the policies of financial liberalization that the *Financial Times* had been trumpeting for the last three decades, and even whether a private banking system was now more costly to capitalism than it was worth.

The Washington overseers of financial markets were equally suffering from policy angst. Former Federal Reserve Chairman Alan Greenspan, the leading free market tribune for bank deregulation in Washington for two decades, speaking before the House Oversight Committee conceded that:

> [T]hose of us who have looked to the self-interest of lending institutions to protect shareholder's equity (myself especially) are in a state of shocked disbelief... To exist you need an ideology. The question is whether it is accurate or not. And what I'm saying to you is 'yes, I have found a flaw.' I don't know how significant or permanent it is. But I have been very distressed by that fact... A flaw in the model that I perceived is the critical functioning structure that defines how the world works, so to speak.[1]

From his perch at the Federal Reserve, Chairman Ben Bernanke, who was de facto in charge of world efforts to cauterize the financial bleeding from becoming a cataclysmic world slump, defended the state takeover of insurance giant AIG, claiming "its failure could have triggered a 1930s-style global financial and economic meltdown, with catastrophic implications for production, incomes, and jobs."[2]

But almost as soon as the serious questioning of capitalism started receiving mainstream media attention, the financial storm eased. As 2009 unfolded, signs of recovery appeared after the unprecedented blast of liquidity into the economy from public loans to the financial sector, the fiscal stimulus and a monetary policy that locked in near-zero interest. In the core capitalist countries of North America, Western Europe, and Japan, the spread of bank collapses began to abate. Indeed, Bank of America and Citigroup announced plans to pay back billions of the emergency bailout loans they had received from the government at the height of the financial panic in 2008. In addition, they committed themselves to purchasing warrants held by the government to re-consolidate private equity control of their firms. Money flowed back into equity markets, and global stock exchanges recovered half of the value lost during the crisis.

Is a U.S.-Centered Neoliberal Global Capitalism Over?

It quickly became a common-sense observation among liberal and Left commentators—from the *New York Times* to *The Nation* to *Monthly Review*—that the financial crisis in itself spelled the end of neoliberalism and the pivotal role of the U.S. in the world economy. To single out just one among innumerable such assessments as the crisis unfolded, the well-known journalist Paul Mason boldly put it this way:

> Global capitalism, on the precipice of collapse, has been rescued by the state. The alternative was oblivion.... we are at the start of an un-American century and a system-wide rethink about the deep priorities of the capitalist system.... Basically, neoliberalism is over: as an ideology, as an economic model. The task of working out what comes after is urgent. Those who want to impose social justice and sustainability have a once-in-a-century chance.[3]

Before all the turmoil, capitalism had been on an incredible run—politically and culturally as well as economically—since the crisis of stagnation and inflation the 1970s. The resolution of that crisis in the 1980s required, as economists put it at the time, "reducing expectations" of the kind nurtured by the trade union militancy and welfare state gains of the 1960s, and putting a stop to the profitability crisis this had created amidst increased global competition. This was accomplished via the defeats suffered by trade unionism and working class parties at the hands of what might properly be called capitalist militancy, not only in North America but around the world. The shift in the balance of class forces (which would also come to mean a setback for social movements as a whole) was further encouraged by dramatic technological change, massive industrial restructuring alongside labor market flexibility and the over all market discipline provided by so-called international competitiveness. The intensification of market relations within countries was also accompanied by their spatial expansion to Eastern Europe, China, India, and many other regions. The incorporation of these new regions into the capitalist world market combined an array of new social relations involving massive proletarianization amidst "a world of slums."

That deepening and spread of market relations and the social discipline that goes with them brought with it an enormous increase in economic inequality, permanent working class insecurity and the subsumption of democratic possibilities to profitable accumulation. In the advanced capitalist core, the bulk of the population was now further integrated into and disciplined by market relations through the private pension funds that mobilized workers' savings on the one hand, and through the mortgage and credit markets that loaned them the money to sustain high levels of consumer spending on the other. At the centre of this were the private banking institutions that, after their collapse in the Great Depression, had been nurtured back to health in the postwar decades and then unleashed in the explosion of global financial innovation that has defined the neoliberal era.

A central question raised by the financial crisis that began in the summer of 2007 was whether capitalism's capacity to integrate the mass of people through their incorporation in financial markets has run out of steam. It certainly seemed so for many working class Americans, particularly African-Americans and the many millions of Hispanic migrant workers.[4] A wider devaluation has also hit working class assets through a general decline in housing prices and of the stock and bonds in which workers' retirement savings are invested. It will be many years before American workers will be able to dig themselves out of the social and debt crises they find themselves plunged into. But we know well from the political experiences of the last three decades that the identification of the socio-economic processes of exploitation and growing inequalities is one thing. It is quite another to draw the conclusion that neoliberalism is over. The political conditions that kept neoliberal policies in play for so long have not been exhausted or undone by the crisis.

Many analysts on the Left have claimed that the crisis proves the U.S. empire is on the decline. But this ignores the continuing centrality of the American state in global capitalism. The crisis reconfirmed the world's dependence on the American state and financial system as capital everywhere initially ran to the safe haven of the U.S. Treasury bond. No other state has deep enough financial markets or the sufficient confidence of international capital to be able to replace the U.S. in this respect. And the resolution of this international crisis has rested fundamentally on the actions of the American state in leading a more or less coordinated response. As the Chinese government has said (not surprisingly) it desperately wants guarantees from the U.S. that it won't default on its debt. The Chinese would very much like an IMF-sponsored international reserve currency that wasn't the dollar. But they're saying all this because they are so utterly dependent on holding U.S. Treasury bills for their own monetary stability in a primarily export-oriented economy. This reveals the extent to which the imperial relationships that built today's global capitalism have persisted through the crisis.

To be sure, U.S. power is confronted by a series of very difficult problems. Indeed trying to integrate the leading states of the Global South that are members of the G20—such as China, India, Brazil, and South Africa—into its informal empire may prove to be even more intractable than what the old empires faced with their colonies. But neither Europe (with its presumably more "civilized" capitalism), nor even China (it used to be Japan that was the favorite example) are challenging the American empire. The crisis is not just a U.S. crisis but a crisis of all the capitalist states embedded in the contradictions of a financialized globalization. They are all scrambling to find a way, under the aegis of the American state's umbrella, to manage this crisis. What gets in the way of thinking clearly about Left alternatives today is that people tend to look for somewhere else that's better, somewhere else that's stronger, somewhere else that's autonomous of the American empire. This is a diversion from thinking about what really needs to be done by way of creating the space for the alternatives we need, above all within the heart of the empire.

The theme of U.S. economic decline has in fact held sway as the primary discourse of the broad progressive movement in the U.S. for some time (a variation of a wider theme in socialist theory of capitalism in terminal stagnation and decline).[5] The American defeat in Vietnam, the economic turmoil of the 1970s, and the end of the dollar-based Bretton Woods international monetary system all seemed to indicate that the limits of American capitalism and power had been reached. The neoliberal policies adopted since the 1980s has further raised the spectre of American economic decline as witnessed in faltering economic growth, low productivity advance, "impatient" capital markets, shift from creditor to debtor status, and languishing competitive capacity taking the form of structural current account deficits. A phalanx of texts from the Left, varying widely in analysis and specific political stances, has sustained this theme across the neoliberal era.[6] The inevitable conclusion drawn from them was that the financial crisis proved that only a mass of credit had concealed the long economic decline of American capitalism.

A number of corollary arguments of these texts have, more or less, been intertwined with the theme of a vicious spiral of financialization and U.S. decline. One is that the financial crisis demonstrates the limits of U.S. state capacity to manage economic instability in the interests of the American ruling class as a whole. This inability, in turn, sharpens divisions in the U.S. power bloc with splits thus beginning to surface between financial and industrial capital. Finally, as U.S. decline intensifies from the predatory encumbrances of financialization, a further shift in the relative balance of power can be expected to lead rival states to openly contest U.S. leadership and hegemony: indeed, key East Asian and European states are already crucial to the U.S. meeting its external financing requirements. And rival power centers—even if they are still capitalist—will provide the political room in the interstate system for a diversity of development models to prevail.

Such analyses of U.S. weakness have led to a schizophrenic political agenda for the North American Left trying to navigate the politics of economic decline and respond to the immediacy of the financial crisis.[7] On the one hand, the organizational tasks of the Left are often defined in terms of taking advantage of divisions among the capitalist classes and melding a progressive "producer alliance" between workers and industrialists against finance to re-establish good jobs, regulation, and the pre-eminence of the U.S. economy. The Democratic Party is usually seen as the obvious organizational vehicle in which such a program could be struck, despite its own linkages with Wall Street. On the other hand, with U.S. capitalism purportedly in decay, it is presumed that the organizational template for effective political action is already in place, so that the North American Left needs only to deepen the existing lines of political resistance to ensure a continuing weakening of the American capitalist class and state.

The reasons why such arguments appear plausible are not hard to find. It is impossible not to look skeptically at neoliberal claims that liberalizing markets will lead to prosperity for all or, in the "third way" variant of this, that introduction of markets to public services will make them more efficient and thus protect them. It is equally unconvincing now to argue that financial self-regulation and innovation will increase economic stability by spreading risk, or that flexible labor markets and de-unionized workplaces will improve job security. And even the belief that increasing dependence on capitalist markets means a parallel increase in democracy, freedom, and equality is no longer credible. The crisis has shown these neoliberal claims to be ideological rubbish.

To take hope that the current dilemmas of global capitalism will lead to a faltering of the American empire is also understandable. U.S. finance appears today as no more than high-flying speculation—

absurdly wasteful and ultimately not sustainable. U.S. corporations and banks may be regaining profitability, but with the household credit crunch and government debt piling up, this is a fragile economic foundation. The capacity of the U.S. state to keep its own house in order is deeply in doubt. The capacity of the U.S. state to impose its policy views for the re-regulation of the world market is, it would appear, equally discredited.

Yet, it is far too easy to assume that the political openings created by the financial crisis will be filled by new rivals for global capitalist leadership and an emerging domestic opposition to American capitalism, each advancing economic alternatives to financialization and neoliberalism. There is a need for a proper political accounting of just how deep are the cracks in the American power structure. We have insisted that a careful reading of the crisis needs to avoid starting from the prejudice that the American state and capitalism are "too weak." This is a view that has a long history on the North American Left. It has led to many misguided efforts of defining a supposedly "progressive agenda" for revitalizing American capitalism, advanced most recently by Joseph Stiglitz.[8] But this reflects a severe underestimation of the economic strengths and the political capabilities of the American state and its ruling classes. It is these enduring capacities—uncontested inside the American state because of the disorganization of the Left and working class politics, as we shall see in the following chapters—that leave the door quite open for a reconstruction of neoliberalism in the next few years, in its class substance if not in all its particular policies.

A continuing awareness of the depth of U.S. imperial power across the inter-state system must remain a central component in the political calculations of the Left around the world. The importance of the U.S. state to the making of neoliberalism and the world market as it exists today should already have once and for all dispelled the illusion that capitalist markets can thrive without state intervention. It was through the types of policies the U.S. advanced to promote free capital movements, international property rights, and labor market flexibility that the era of free trade and globalization was unleashed. And this era has been kept going as long as it has by the repeated coordinated interventions undertaken by central banks and finance ministries, under the political leadership of the Federal Reserve and the American Treasury, to contain the periodic crises to which such a volatile system of global finance inevitably gives rise. To this end, as we show, the

Federal Reserve has acted very much like the world's central bank and poured liquidity into the U.S. financial system and coordinated other central banks in similar efforts.

The U.S. budgetary position of sustained trillion dollar deficits—so often invoked, along with trade deficits, as a direct measure for apocalyptic forecasts of decline—also needs to seen in a more sober perspective. The U.S. fiscal position is, in fact, still quite far from the debt loads being carried by Japan and many other core capitalist countries, and they remain quite far below the debt levels sustained by the U.S. at the end of World War II. This is the case even though the U.S. has one of the lowest overall tax burdens among core countries and does not have a national value-added tax. In any case, the U.S. fiscal deficit should not be interpreted as a direct correlate of economic decline. It measures, in one sense, the capacity of the U.S. ruling class to avoid further taxes themselves and to pass the burden onto the American working classes, which gives U.S. capitalists distinct competitive advantages compared to most others in the core countries. The deficit also reflects the global imbalances that involve the U.S. acting as the primary world consumer and absorber of global savings.

The deficit also needs to be seen in relation to whether it involves public expenditure that pertains to rebuilding infrastructure, which has the potential to boost competitiveness. The collapsed levees of New Orleans and the buckling bridges of Minneapolis dramatically showed the long-neglected need to rebuild U.S. infrastructure, and this is now reinforced by strategies for new capital accumulation via supporting alternative energy development. The type of state intervention that supported financial globalization is not well suited to this, but the crisis can lead to a renewal of neglected state capacities and borrowing for these purposes can be justified apart from the need for emergency fiscal stimulus.

And even with a broad consensus after the crisis that finance needs more regulation, it must be recognized that this in itself would not necessarily spell the end to the kind of financialization, which as we shall see, has been so essential to the making and reproduction of global capitalism under American leadership. The processes that constitute financialization are in fact likely to be reconceived in ways designed to ensure that finance can continue to be "innovative" and still diversify risk. The greater regulatory oversight of financial markets being proposed is meant to improve the transparency and efficiency of the new innovations, not abolish them. The "Americanization" of global finance, both as the emulation by other countries of U.S. financial practices and as their penetration by U.S. banks, is an advantage the U.S. has long exploited to the benefit of its ruling classes. It would be reckless to suggest these advantages have simply vanished without the American capitalist classes doing everything in their power, and mobilizing the power of the U.S. state as part of such an effort, to restore them.

Finally, it is important to grasp the fact that no major state has seen the crisis as an opportunity to challenge or undermine the American state. Rather, the integration of global capitalism has meant that there has been extensive international coordination across states in the provision of liquidity to financial system, in fiscal stimulus, the avoidance of a massive resort to tariff wars, and in beginning to establish new regulatory regimes for finance. The penetration by American finance of foreign countries and the inflow of foreign capital into the U.S. has given it access to global savings, shored up its role as the greatest global consumer and reinforced the U.S. state's power and options. Through the crisis and now in a phase of recovery, no alternative configuration of the world market has emerged to address these imbalances or to supersede the U.S. economy—and U.S. finance—at the centre of global power structures. Rather than occurring at the level of inter-state antagonisms, competitive rivalries have long taken the form of competition among multinational corporations that operate within each other's states, and are key actors in the class struggles over wages, social programs, taxation, economic restructuring within them.

There may well be some loss of appeal of U.S. leadership (with the military quagmire in Afghanistan an added factor) and some modulations in relative power in the inter-state system. But it would be utterly foolish to think that the U.S. imperium will be readily displaced from the centre of political attention as the foremost obstacle to transforming the world system. To posit a terminal decline in U.S. imperial power is to attempt to accomplish in theory what remains to be done in political struggle. The "exit strategies" from the emergency state interventions during the crisis now being debated by governments—with the IMF and various other agencies suggesting a decade of austerity is coming—may test the legitimacy of a U.S.-centered global capitalism, but they hardly determine its demise.[9]

In the Global South, as even in Greece today, structural adjustment programs that the IMF so widely imposed for decades to secure free capital flows, domestic market liberalization, and social austerity are also not about to go away, even if it is likely they will be popularly contested. Nor is globalization going away. The crisis highlighted the importance of expanding the meetings of the Group of Seven (G7) core capitalist states to the wider pivotal Group of Twenty that included the leading capitalist states of the Global South. The G20 meetings during the crisis accomplished little in concrete policy terms, but they did confirm a commitment among the participating states to keep the internationalization of capital going through free trade and foreign investment. The American state's central role in organizing and setting the agenda at these G20 meetings shows that while the U.S. empire may have lost some of its sheen in the crisis, here, too, the reality is not an imminent end to the American empire and the reversal of its leadership role.

The North American Left's Political Contours

The strategically most important questions for the Left, therefore, go beyond the economic dimensions of the crisis to its political contours. What lessons will the ruling class draw from the financial crisis and how will they calibrate their political options? How will the working class respond to the crisis? If credit becomes more costly; if the loss of private pensions, negotiated healthcare benefits and the loss of home values force people into having to reduce consumption to shore up their savings; and if food and oil price increases leave less discretionary spending, will working class people organize politically and rebel? Or will workers once again tighten their belts to preserve what is left from their past gains as another decade of wage and public sector austerity presses forward?

The financial crisis has seemingly changed everything in North America and yet nothing has changed. The crisis has not led the various elements that compose the capitalist classes by state, region, sector, size to turn upon each other, with contesting policy agendas that reflect divisions subordinate classes might exploit. This intra-class unity has been crucial to the capacity of capitalist states to contain the crisis. As governments from California to Ontario, whatever their color, attempt to cope with their deficits, kick-start accumulation, and underwrite a credit expansion, they are effectively involved in reconstructing the neoliberal political project. The "exit strategies" being mooted by these governments all have the working classes paying for the crisis, particularly via increases in austerity in wages and pensions, payroll and consumption taxes, and cuts in public services. If the ghosts of the extended revolts of the 1960s that made it so hard to quickly resolve the crisis of the 1970s continues to haunt ruling elites, this is mainly seen in their stiff determination to quickly resolve today's crisis today on their own terms. More authoritarian political relations in both workplaces and the state may well be a consequence of this very aggressive, militant, and confident capitalist strategy.

In the wake of the North American Left's failure to develop lasting and effective political vehicles in the course of opposing neoliberalism over the last three decades, political resistance to the financial crisis has so far been largely spontaneous and sporadic. This has been registered in outbursts of direct action in reclaiming and occupying houses amongst anti-poverty and shelter activists in various cities from Miami to Vancouver; factory occupations by workers demanding proper severances and pensions, from Republic Windows in Chicago and to the Aradco auto plant in Windsor; the rejection of further concession demands by employers, from rank and file Ford workers to the sustained strike of miners against Vale-Inco in Sudbury; and the student and teacher revolt against university cutbacks across California.[10]

As crucial as spontaneous resistance is for any progressive change, there has not been the degree of political organization necessary to be effective and to be sustained. The sporadic outbursts have been almost entirely defensive, while most of the inherited forms that constrained effective political opposition to neoliberalism have been reinforced through this crisis, such as "plain and simple" trade unionism in defense of jobs alone; narrow public interest lobbying of legislators on the details of the bailout package; and the misconceived call for regulation of the financial sector as the focus of political work. All this points to the remarkable "flexibility" that the U.S. state and ruling classes have had in terms of the resolution of the crisis, as well as the basic weakness of the Left. This has given it additional room for maneuver in the world market in coordinating and negotiating the international response to the crisis.

This crisis saw the greatest concessions U.S. autoworkers have ever made by the United Auto Workers union, once the linchpin of the U.S. labor movement. The impact of these concessions is now spreading across North American working classes. That the outgoing Bush administration was able to leverage the auto crisis to all but destroy the UAW as an independent social force—with the Obama Administration doing nothing to reverse it—is a telling example of how the ruling classes will exploit a crisis to their own advantage. For example, had U.S. unions been determined and strong enough to resist concessions and secure compensation for the decline of the value of their homes and pensions, the policies adopted by the U.S. government would have been quite different. Instead, wage restraint and social austerity have gained ground.

This helps explain why North American ruling classes have not been divided around what type of regulation to impose on financial markets. They have been able to take advantage of labor market insecurities and rewrite collective bargaining agreements while the American state finds new ways to reconstitute neoliberalism globally. Elements of finance may still be in disarray, but the ruling classes in the U.S. and across North America have the resources, power and the organizational support of the state to restructure and recast and pursue their political interests. Labor and the Left more broadly in North America are currently bereft of any comparable strategic resources. Certain economic crises in the past, the Great Depression of the 1930s above all, have created openings and opportunities for *both* capitalists and workers. But in the absence of an organizational infrastructure for resistance, which can sustain struggles through time and transmit them across communities, such labor and Left opposition as does emerge is likely to be contained and localized rather than be the basis for developing new political capacities.

The following chapters seek to make a contribution towards clarifying what needs doing, beginning in Chapter 2 by dispelling some debilitating misconceptions on the Left concerning the nature of capitalist crises as well as the relationship between the state, finance and production in the neoliberal era. Chapter 3 traces the historical process through which, over a century punctuated by previous crises, the American state and finance developed in tandem, and came to play a new kind of imperial role at the center of global capitalism. And in light of the contradictions that were produced in this process, Chapter 4 traces the development of the crisis that began in 2007 and explains the active role of the American state, both under Bush and Obama, in containing the crisis in ways that reproduced the structures of class inequality and power domestically and internationally.

Turning in Chapter 5 to an analysis of how the relationship between industry and finance played itself out in the crisis in the auto sector, the full class dimensions of the crisis are brought to the fore; this leads to a sober examination in Chapter 6 of the impasse of the North American labor movement and how seriously this affects the North American Left. The remit of Chapter 7 is to try to think creatively about alternatives, not least in terms of how advancing the case for democratic economic planning, including via nationalization of the banks and the auto industry, must become integrated with demands for immediate reforms. The realization of such alternatives will require the development of the kinds of labor, community, and political movements that can embody the organizational as well as educational and programmatic capacities that are critical for unleashing the popular powers necessary for a truly democratic economy and state. The concluding chapter distils our overall argument by presenting in thesis form our conceptualization of the neoliberal period of capitalism, our reading of the crisis, and the vision and politics behind the strategic alternatives this book advances for the North American Left.

CHAPTER TWO

NEOLIBERALISM, FINANCE, AND CRISES

Since at least the election of Ronald Reagan in 1980, the U.S. and other states have embraced an ideology of scaling back the role of government in economic life and letting the invisible hand of the unfettered market work its magic. Rhetoric notwithstanding, this has *not* meant a withdrawal of the state from regulating economic activity nor from an active role in managing class relations. Instead, it has signaled the institutionalization of public policies and state regulation directed at increasing the power of the dominant capitalist firms in industry as well as financial markets and an enhanced role for markets in determining income distribution and public priorities. This political project has become associated in all parts of the world with the term neoliberalism—a term now of general derision amongst vast swathes of the world's population. One of its central ideologues, Thomas Friedman of the *New York Times*, provided the classic popular characterization of the policy agenda:

> a country must either adopt, or be seen as moving toward, the following golden rules: making the private sector the primary engine of its economic growth, maintaining a low rate of inflation and price stability, shrinking the size of its state bureaucracy, maintaining as close to a balanced budget as possible, if not a

> surplus, eliminating and lowering tariffs on imported goods, removing restrictions on foreign investment, getting rid of quotas and domestic monopolies, increasing exports, privatizing state-owned industries and utilities, deregulating capital markets, making its currency convertible, opening its industries, stock and bond markets to direct foreign ownership and investment, deregulating its economy to promote as much domestic competition as possible, eliminating government corruption, subsidies and kickbacks as possible, opening its banking and telecommunications systems to private ownership and competition, and allowing its citizens to choose from an array of competing pension options and foreign-run pension and mutual funds.[11]

Neoliberalism's "golden rules" have had the objectives of expanding the reach of capitalist markets, captured in popular discourse by the term globalization. The policy rules have also had the intent to "narrow the political and economic choices of those in power" such that "policy choices get reduced to Pepsi or Coke."[12] The successful pursuit of these objectives has been the particular triumph of the American state. Neoliberalism is not, in our view, about the extent of deregulation as opposed to regulation, or holding on tenaciously to this or that public policy component. Neoliberalism should be understood as a particular form of class rule and state power that intensifies competitive imperatives for both firms and workers, increases dependence on the market in daily life and reinforces the dominant hierarchies of the world market, with the U.S. at its apex.

From this background, it is possible to identify a linkage between neoliberalism and the greater absolute place that finance occupies in overall economic activity. What is called financialization involves not only credit markets playing a more pivotal role in the capitalist economy, but also economic development that is increasingly "finance-led" in terms of the corporate decisions that determine investment flows and even the decisions individuals and households make in meeting their needs. Finance's enhanced place in the political alliances of capital and, in the power structures of the state, has gained it a more determining role in the shaping of government policy.

The financial excesses that triggered the Great Recession, with the continual revelations of wanton greed and corruption at the summits of American finance, could not but raise serious questioning of the course of American capitalism over the last decades. Indeed, a massive populist hostility—from the "tea-baggers" on the Right madly protesting Obama's "socialism," to the popularity of Michael Moore's acidic comedy, *Capitalism: A Love Story*, to riveting recounts of the shamelessness of the American plutocracy—came pouring out[13]. This enmity has focused particularly on Wall Street and the banks, but often has also been directed toward neoliberalism and even against capitalism itself.

In response, the neoliberals urgently offered up a panoply of diagnoses of where the errors had occurred and what new bulwarks to stabilize financial markets were needed. A rigorous defense of free-market capitalism was required, precisely because so much more was at stake than Wall Street's status and the survival of some of its venerable banks, not the least of which was to protect as best they could what they had managed to consolidate over three decades.

A few prominent lines of defense quickly emerged, each quite predictably invoking government as the malevolent actor upsetting otherwise efficient exchanges and innovations occurring in financial markets.[14] One was that the government had encouraged the establishment of "mistaken incentive" structures for financial firms that then lent themselves to the abuses of "moral hazard"—the neoliberal term for malfeasance—by the adoption of corporate governance structures that pivoted around "performance-based compensation." With financial transactions generating huge bonuses (with Initial Public Offerings or IPOs and various kinds of leveraged buyouts being particularly lucrative), executives, traders and brokers all had enormous incentives to take on high-risk, high-leverage positions with no one—bankers themselves, regulators, rating agencies, shareholders—adequately monitoring firm liquidity. The monetary authorities, moreover, actively promoted individual and corporate moral hazard by backstopping losses and thus allowing the shirking of responsibility for the risks being borne, especially by off-loading debt into the "shadow banking system." It became quite rational for financiers to game the system, so the argument went, because at the end of the day governments would bail-out firms "too big to fail" and the bonuses received from high-risk ventures would always outstrip the losses from failed loans.

A second line of defense has been that ill-understood financial products—such as adjustable rate mortgages, teaser rates, opaque credit card incentives for consumers, and an array of derivates, such as collaterized debt obligations (CDOs) to spread risk among lenders—generated 'false price signals'. Borrowers seldom understood the actual "prices" they were paying. In these new markets, knowledge and clear prices were in severe shortage, but the Federal Reserve and the Securities and Exchange Commission (SEC) did next nothing to ensure appropriate price transparency. Moreover, Congress actively encouraged the spread of these exchanges by mandating creditors to invest in "high-risk"—meaning low-income, high unemployment—communities while also endorsing the new financial instruments and higher leverage ratios of loans to available capital.

A third line of defense takes these critiques a step further and blames explicit government monetary policy errors which stoked an "asset-inflation credit bubble" by lowering interest rates to unsustainable levels from 2001–2005 in response to the dot-com and 9/11 stock market collapses. Just as the Federal Reserve was blamed for raising interest rates instead of lowering them after the 1929 stock market crash, it was now said the Fed was to blame for having lowered interest rates after the collapse of the dot.com stock market bubble at the turn of the millennium. As a result, rather than a "normal" market correction of inflated asset prices, they set the stage for a huge crisis in the global financial system.

There may well be some merit to these analyses. Poorly regulated and under-institutionalized markets are, indeed, prime conditions for all-out speculative fervor. Karl Marx noted that "credit... suspends [the] barriers to the realization of capital only by raising them to their most general form."[15] At the end of the day, however, these defenses are all modernized versions of the old theory that was used to pin the causes of the Great Depression on government policy, diverting attention away from the actions of Wall Street financiers—let alone any of the inherent crisis tendencies in capitalist finance.[16]

These defenses proceed from a deep-seated—perhaps deliberately so?—theoretical misconception. This lies in the crude distinction they make between a potentially enclosed self-regulating sphere of efficient markets and a separate sphere of political perversity and interfering states. Regulatory failures, moral hazards, improper alignment of incentive structures, and so forth all supposedly arise from rational actors falling victim to destabilizing political impositions—with banks, hedge funds and other financial institutions the most rational market calculating machines of all.

Recognizing the brittleness of these neoliberal defenses of finance, the arch-conservative Niall Ferguson, Harvard business historian, financial commentator, and author of *The Ascent of Money* (2008), took quite the opposite tack. Instead of seeing the state as a disruptive imposition on financial markets, he revived the old Marxist arguments, last popularized by Communist parties in the 1950s, of a malignant direct fusion between the state and finance and identified state-monopoly capitalism as the culprit. "I wholly share Lenin's view that the rise to power of a financial oligarchy is undesirable and should be as far as possible a transient phenomenon," he contended. "The question is how we can extricate ourselves from Stamokap and return to the capitalism of free competition."[17] Ferguson's conclusion is surely a flight of fancy and a convoluted effort to defend banks and bankers. But at least it does not evade the need to examine the linkages between financial power and state power. A closer look at the state regulatory structures that underpinned the hypertrophy of financial capital in both its market dynamics and its political power under neoliberalism is clearly warranted.

Challenging Financial Capitalism

It needs to be noted upfront that hardly any element of the Left—in North America, but it is possible to claim even globally—could be accused of being taken completely by surprise by the financial crisis. A defining feature of progressive politics in North America, from the late 19th century to Hyman Minsky and Doug Henwood in the late 20th, has been the denunciation of the monopolies and banks of Wall Street and Bay Street.[18] This was also important in framing the politics of the New Deal and the regulatory policies on finance adopted at that time. Before and after the "Battle of Seattle" in 1999, the anti-globalization movement has sustained sharp critiques of neoliberal financial policies—from the structural adjustment policies of the IMF to the campaigns against the Multilateral Agreement on Investment and bank deregulation and to persistent calls for a Tobin Tax on financial transactions.

These critiques—Henwood aside—have generally focused on financial instability emerging from an institutional mismatch between state regulatory policies and new forms of financial accumulation damaging the "real" economy. They have animated the prevailing vision of the financial crisis amongst the progressive movement in the U.S. and the programmatic agenda in opposition to financial capitalism. Their varying views need to be fleshed out a bit more.

One critique of financial capitalism, particularly associated with prominent liberal financial commentators like Paul Krugman and Joseph Stiglitz, points to "regulatory gaps" between state regulators and financial markets.[19] Neoliberal policies abet market instabilities that are caused by the unequal distribution of information, especially by allowing bankers and other financial agents to move into hedging and speculative activities and away from defined roles as lenders, insurers, brokers, and so on. Insofar is this was the cause of the crisis, government intervention via bank bailouts, interest rate cuts and fiscal stimulus can treat the symptoms but not serve as the cure. Strong markets—including strong financial markets—need to be counterbalanced by a robust regulatory state.

The critique is taken a significant step further if, following Minsky as Paul Mason and Robert Wade have done, the tendency of financial agents to increase speculative arbitrage is not seen as something emerging from regulatory gaps, but occurs as part of the "systematic dynamics" internal to financial markets.[20] Given a reinforcing cycle of credit and speculation, asset values inflate and bubbles unavoidably form. Any economic contraction, caused by an industrial slowdown or an increase in interest rates, will trigger the undoing of some hedges on the risk that financial agents have taken and it is really just a question of how far they ripple through the financial system that determines how deep and wide any ensuing crisis will be. Neoliberal policies have only reinforced these financial dynamics, rather than caused them. They have however contributed to the forming the "mother of all bubbles" by allowing for the unregulated financial innovations and excesses of the last decade.

A third critique, long advanced by *Monthly Review*'s Marxist economists, and more recently by Andrew Glyn, Giovanni Arrighi and Robert Brenner, is quite distinct in its analysis and political agenda, but parallels the above critiques in seeing financialization as a symptom of decline of the "real" productive economy.[21] The financial and credit policies of neoliberalism fail to address underlying problems of overcapacity and low productivity by bolstering effective demand and preventing a cleansing of the economy to provide a stable foundation for renewed accumulation. Lower interest rates and the availability of credit to consumers and businesses provide relief from these problems but at the cost of generating ever-larger financial bubbles, as long as the unresolved underlying overaccumulation problem remains in place.

While the insights from these analyses are many, and the views vary considerably, a few common and serious misconceptions have pervaded progressive accounts of the crisis. First, since financialization is mainly seen as a response to the lack of investment opportunities in productive sectors, this misrepresents what has actually been a very dynamic period of capitalism. This has involved the penetration of capitalist social relations into new spheres by way of the massive organizational restructuring of the workplace, companies, and sectors; the deployment of new technologies and breakthroughs into new fields for capital accumulation; the penetration and expansion of markets and corporations into geographic spaces previously excluded; the "flexibilization" of labor and the lowering of working-class wages, rights and expectations—all supported by an accompanying overhaul of state administration. Many of the innovations in finance have in fact facilitated this restructuring in systems of production and spread them through the internationalization of capital.

It is indeed the case that the levels of financialization—taken to unsustainable levels in their existing forms—and the forms of financial innovation—taken to Byzantine complexity—are quite central to the evolution of neoliberalism and integral to the character of the current crisis. But it is quite inadequate to pose this strictly, in the first instance, as an opposition between a predatory financial sector and a productive economy, and, in the second, as an unstable means to prop up a stagnant economy. This too often slips into the conceptual and political—reductionism that speculative/fictitious capital, depending upon the theoretical framework, equals a speculative/fictitious economy.

This is to draw the conclusion before the analysis. It is to treat the financial sphere as a "superstructure" wholly dependent upon a "material base" in the real economy.[22] This is a false dichotomy. Money capital, bank capital, credit and speculative capital are all necessary moments in the circuits of capitalist production and exchange. Capitalism is inconceivable without them, as all individual capitalists must put up their capital in advance and speculate that their commodities can be sold and a profit earned in the future. "Fictitious capital" and indeed all the credit generated by the financial system is inherent in the money-form and a necessary part of capitalist accumulation, even if ultimately dependent on the "real" economy for its revenues (that is, capitalism rests on the production of commodities not just their circulation).

The "fictitious capital" generated in financial markets is not purely speculative in the sense that playing slot machines in a casino is speculative. Behind a new firm or a new product rests the 'speculation' that it can be sold at a cost and price that generates profit. The populist distinction between the financial and "productive" sectors relies on a one-sided notion that finance speculates in pieces of paper, and not in providing real goods and services. The problem with this line of thinking is that it mistakes what is rational from the perspective of certain moral criteria with what is rational *within capitalism.* The financial system is necessary to capitalism's functioning, and innovations in financial markets provide competitive advantages for the originating capitals and the states they reside in. The discipline finance has imposed in the neoliberal era on particular capitalists and workers has forced, moreover, an increase in U.S. productivity rates by way of increased exploitation, the more intense use of each unit of capital, and the reallocation of capital to sectors that are more promising. Financial markets have come to provide non-financial corporations with mechanisms for managing their risks, and comparing and evaluating diverse investment opportunities in a highly complex global economy. This perspective on private banking systems is, of course, from the standpoint of capitalist profits and power. But it is why the irrational exuberances and speculative excesses that are also fuelled by finance are allowed to be repeated time and again. Absent this cost, globalization—at least in terms of how it has actually evolved—would not have been possible.

Financial capital, moreover, plays a dominant economic role in pooling the social surplus, creating credit-money in advance of production, disciplining wayward firms by withholding credit and in determining what new branches of industry to channel new investments. This role has important political and ideological effects in cementing political alliances amongst blocs of capital and forwarding ideological agendas that defend market exchanges and profit-making as a whole. Quite the contrary to being a predatory breed of capitalists picking over the successes and ruins of a productive economy, financial capital represents and defends the interests of all capitalists in capitalism.

The fault-line internal to financial capital of breeding financial crises and speculative bubbles—in the pursuit, as Marx phrased it, of "money begetting money"—must be interpreted with these integral features in mind. This is the key to unlocking a central paradox of neoliberalism within American capitalism: *financialization gives rise to such financial volatility that crises actually become one of the developmental features of neoliberalism, and this reinforces rather than undermines the central position of financial interests in capitalist power structures.*

A further misconception concerns the nature of state regulation. Since financial markets are seen as inadequately supervised, with regulatory reckless risk-taking actually encouraged by regulatory agencies, this raises analytical and political questions about what form regulation should take to displace the ill-advised policies of neoliberalism. Yet the fundamental relationship between capitalist states and financial markets cannot be understood in terms of how much or little regulation the former puts upon the latter. Neoliberalism brought a change in the mode of regulation, but there wasn't less regulation. Moreover, freer markets often require more rules, if nothing else to protect the property owners who are in the market, to lay the rules under which they can sue each other and go to court when they are not able to make their obligations. It is certainly possible to say that the regulatory agencies should have developed forms of controlling some of the rampant speculative and fraudulent activities. But regulatory agencies weren't interested in that. Their role was developing the kinds of regulations that would promote financial innovation. And the resultant financial speculation has been central to the kind of dynamic globalization that capitalism produced to the cost of a great many people around the world, especially in the Global South.

These misconceptions at the level of analysis have resulted, more often than not, in a series of mistaken expectations of the course of American capitalism and thus the forms that political opposition to the financial crisis might take. It is, for example, far too early to proclaim that neoliberalism has come to an end as many progressives in North America quickly slipped into declaring. It is crucial to distinguish between neoliberalism as an *ideologically-driven strategy to free markets from states*, and as a *materially-driven form of social practices and rules* which has required state intervention and management to liberalize markets. New state practices and regulations within capitalism have been adopted in the midst of the crisis. But new regulations by themselves may only help reconstitute neoliberal inequalities and power structures on a new foundation, unless there is a fundamental shift in the balance of class forces.

The analytical differences with neoliberals over the appropriate regulatory structures to impose on financial capital often slides, in many analyses by progressives, into the expectation of a political division between finance and industry. Indeed, this is a legacy in North American populism, the Popular Front and business unionism, posing a political opposition between the interests of the "producers" against the interests of the speculative "money-lenders." Yet, financial capital has barely sacrificed any of its access to the centers of political power over the course of the crisis. And despite the fierce debates about how to address the financial crisis, and the profound restructuring in the auto, electronics, pulp and paper and steel sectors, manufacturing capital in North America has offered neither a political nor a policy alternative to the strategies of Wall Street. There is a measure of political dissent in Washington amongst the Democrats and, from a different angle, the right-wing of the Republican Party. But it is pure fantasy to see significant splits between different sections of the capitalist classes or a fracturing of political parties, beyond the typical jockeying of interests that would alter the trajectory of American capitalism.

The view of finance as speculative is usually twinned with the assessment that U.S. political power is in terminal decline. In the context of a financial crisis centered in the U.S. "heartland" of the world market, major divisions within the inter-state system could be expected to burst forward. But even in the context of geopolitical rivalries over regional interests, and international competition over how the burden of financial losses will be distributed internationally, new forms of political coordination have materialized to encompass the G20 group of states, as well as new bilateral operational relations between China and the U.S. *The crisis of the empire is a crisis of all the capitalist states in the empire.* There is not, in that sense, a direct relative loss of American power. There are enormous problems that the contradictions of a financialized globalization under U.S. leadership got them all into. But it is also under the American state's umbrella that they are attempting to manage their way out of the crisis.

The Left needs to come to grips with the political consequence of this: there has been no significant disunity amongst the main fractions of capital—between industrial capital and finance, between foreign and national capitals, and between big and small capitals. They have all seen their political stake in the resolution of the crisis in a way which reconstitutes neoliberal hegemony. This is remarkable given what we know of the history of major crises in the past.

A misreading of the balance of political forces within the ruling blocs and the inter-state system has also led to the mistaken prognosis that the discrediting of neoliberalism will give rise to spontaneous opposition from there to an alternate governing coalition. The lesson learned by many sections of the North American ruling classes, however, has not only been one of market failures being compensated by appropriate regulation, but the possibility to even further rewrite collective bargaining agreements and to find new ways to prop up the neoliberal state.

Rather than witnessing a shift in the balance of class forces toward workers and popular movements, the course of the crisis has favored the capitalist classes. Indeed, the worst features of the inherited forms of political opposition have been reinforced, from business unionism to narrow lobbying of legislators as the focus of political work—across North America. Economic crises feed the politics that exist. If the Left is disorganized and marginalized—and this is one of the central accomplishments of neoliberalism in North America—alternate political programs and the disorganization of the working class and progressive movements will not be reversed by the force of the crisis itself.

Thinking about Crises

In interpreting such a many-sided process, it is easy enough to point to the various shortcomings and pitfalls in analyses of the crisis. A good deal of clarifying positions and collective learning can occur from such efforts. However, it is just as or more important to put forward alternate explanations to uncover unexpected linkages, identify other factors influencing developments and offer a political strategy for a route forward for North American workers.

To begin with, the meaning of crisis adopted for the purposes at hand here should be noted, as it has been the subject of endless—sometimes insightful—controversy within radical political economy, particularly with respect to understanding the current phase of capitalism commonly referred to as neoliberal globalization. We start from a fundamental contradiction between the competitive imperative that drives capitalists to accumulate money-capital *without limit*, yet at the same time constrains them by having to organize the productive forces they employ *within the limits* of profitability.

This raises a second crucial contradiction. Capital always seeks to invest and accumulate beyond local and national boundaries yet remains embedded in and dependent on the national form of the state in the international state system. This tension between the international character of capital accumulation and the nation-state is key to understanding crises as they actually exist in history and are struggled over by social classes. Capitalist markets do not exist externally from states; they are intrinsic to the formation and operation of markets. Nor are states extraneous to crises. They are implicated in both how they emerge and how they are resolved, as well as in managing their political impact within the international state system.

All crises of capitalism are, in this sense, crises of overaccumulation. Capital as a whole—or some branches of industry or specific firms—has accumulated to an extent that the surplus value (profits) being extracted from workers and the stream of revenues flowing to capitalists from sales is not high enough—whether due to a wage-squeeze, a decline in the productivity of the capital stock, or adequate effective demand in the economy— relative to the investments made to sustain an adequate level of *profitability*. Without profits, capital cannot continue to expand and a crisis unfolds. In *The Communist Manifesto*, Marx and Engels already contended that

> the history of industry and commerce is but the history of the revolt of modern productive forces against modern conditions of production... In these crises a great part not only of the existing products, but also of the previously created productive forces, are periodically destroyed... In these crises there breaks out an epidemic that, in all earlier epochs, would have seemed an absurdity—the epidemic of overproduction... Because there is too much civilization, too much means of subsistence, too much industry, too much commerce.[23]

As important as it is to understand capitalism's constant drive to over-accumulation as a fundamental characteristic of capitalism, it does not, however, get us very far in penetrating a particular phase of capitalism. Several crucial questions about crises as historical events are left to be answered, such as the timing, causes and dynamics of specific crises, and the circumstances in which these specific crises are overcome. Marx's famous argument of a tendency towards a falling rate of profit in the third volume of *Capital*, for example, does not provide a general theory of crises (although it is often invoked as such) or a particular guide to the analysis of political conjunctures (although even here it is sometimes proposed as orthodox arbiter of dispute). The fall in the rate of profit caused by the capitalist developmental "tendency" to increase the size of investments and the build up of more and more capital stock is offset by a series of "counter-tendencies" to increase productivity, and exploit new markets and resources. "These various influences sometimes tend to exhibit themselves side by side, spatially; at other times, one after another, temporally. And at certain times the conflict of contending agencies breaks through in crises. Crises are never more than momentary, violent solutions for the existing contradictions, violent eruptions that re-establish the disturbed balance for the time being."[24] As Marx argues, the counter-tendencies are, as often as not, the very substance of capitalism's dynamics. They are exhibited in higher rates of class exploitation, the development of new internal markets, new technologies altering the capital stock, international expansion of the circuits of capital, credit multiplying in all its forms, and state intervention directly into the relations of production.

These abstract ideas point to the importance of the restructuring of capital as an elemental characteristic of accumulation—the competitive imperatives that compel each capitalist "to keep extending [their] capital in order to preserve it."[25] But the laws of development, to the extent we can use that phrase in a strong sense, cannot be mechanically interpreted so as to expunge class struggle and politics from our analysis. There can be a general theory of capitalist development and the contradictions which lead to recurrent instability and crises within capitalism, but a "law of crisis" cannot be drawn across the history of capitalism.

The interesting *political* questions relate not only to *why* crises occur under capitalism, but also as to what makes each crisis *distinct*: why do crises erupt; why do they linger; why do the class struggles in response to crises take the form they do? In what way is the state modifying its form and adapting the functions of the state apparatuses? And what political openings and transformations are appearing on the agenda? It is these political questions that preoccupy us in this book. It might be helpful to draw a few themes out a bit more.

First, in the political characteristics they take, crises are *historically specific*. They occur within a particular period of capitalist development and must be theorized within the class and institutional contradictions of that period. Crises will always have particular causes and confronting them will involve overcoming particular barriers to the further accumulation of capital. Moreover, this will be affected by the specific form of the state that is implicated in any particular crisis and by the distinct ways the crisis spreads through the state system, given patterns of uneven development. The weakness, for example, of applying a general theory of crisis that tries to encompass the crises at the end of the 19th century, the Great Depression of the 1930s, and that of the 1970s and today's financial crisis lies in all that is obscured along the way. This ranges across the radically different degree of proletarianization in each period (in the late 19th century unskilled workers might still return to the land and skilled workers were as or more mobile than industrial capital) and the very distinct organizational form adopted by units of capital (even in the 1930s, the corporate, multidivisional, global, networked form was not yet a gleam in any capitalist's eye). Moreover, the scope of finance and nature of regulation varied enormously, reflecting the relative scale and extent of state capacities as well as the extent of democratization and organized working class power.

Second, in examining crises it is not only a question of why particular crises occur, but also what contradictions and barriers stand in the way of their resolution. The two questions overlap, but are not identical and lead to different lines of thinking. In the midst of a serious disruption of accumulation, it is the uncertainty about its resolution that continues to characterize it as a crisis, often after the economic hemorrhaging has stopped. This uncertainty relates to the explicit *political* contingency of social struggles and whether political alliances can be formed so as to accommodate the resumption of accumulation. It also relates to the *capability* contingency of whether the state in particular—but also capitalist classes in terms of their organizational form and capital utilization—can develop the new institutional infrastructure to support a revival of accumulation.

Third, the internationalization of capital does not mean that crises can be understood apart from the national form of the state.[26] In particular, the law of value—known in modern parlance as international competitiveness in free markets—and the rule of money are constituted through states, so that even the most powerful state is structured so as to protect capitalist interests and property. Financialization increases this subordination not as an external limit imposed by an autonomous world market, but as an internalized set of relations and political norms within national power structures and the form of the state and the internal organization of the various agencies and departments of the state. The role that dominant states play within the inter-state system in disciplining other states in terms of the law of value (as seen in IMF structural adjustment policies) also involves upholding and defending the rule of money (e.g. the convertibility of national currencies and the free movement of capital). The American state's role as the leading state in global capitalism involves developing the distinct regulatory norms that facilitate this not just within its own borders, but also by coordinating politically as well as administratively across the inter-state system.

These conceptual points immediately take us some distance from analyses of financial crises as being due to "policy mistakes and errors" or to governmental "regulatory mismatches" with processes of financial accumulation. General theories of crises can reveal some of the structural features of development, but they too often focus, paradoxically, on patterns of continuity in a few variables, missing new features in contemporary capitalism, and new patterns in class relations and forms of state power. It is the particular context in which this crisis emerges, and its distinct features, that we will highlight in future chapters.[27]

Theories that are too general miss the central feature of contemporary social struggle and political conflict: that the crisis of the 1970s was, from capital's perspective, successfully ended. Missing this point leads to two key errors. It leads to a failure to account for the revival of profit rates, profit shares and real investment from the 1980s into the 1990s—even if they did not reach the historically unique levels of the mid-1960s. This dynamism also includes the new zones for capitalist development in Eastern Europe, Latin America, China, and India.

And analyzing the present crisis through the lens of the 1970s overlooks the radically transformed context from the defeat of the labor movement, at both the point of production over unionization and wages and in realm of politics in forming political alliances and advancing programmatic agendas. This defeat was also the premise underlying the forms that the financialization and the internationalization of capital would take. It is important to take into account here the extent to which finance has been an integral and functional part of capitalist accumulation, providing conditional access to credit for businesses and worker-consumers, disciplining firms through this and through "shareholder value" principles, assessing risk and measuring "value," reallocating capital across sectors and around the world, and in this way reproducing U.S. dominance.

The onset of the crisis in 2007 was not rooted in any sharp profit decline or collapse of investment. In 2006–07, profits were at peak and an investment expansion appeared to be forming—productivity continuing to increase substantially in manufacturing, labor compensation lagging, and low-cost inputs being imported from export processing zones in Mexico and China. Rather it was rooted in the dynamics of finance. In spite of some important exceptions (notably in the "Detroit Three"), American corporations came into this crisis in generally solid financial shape in terms of profits, debt, and cash flow. The present assessment of the U.S. economy needs to take account of both the uneven strength of the U.S. economy—without which the crisis would have been much deeper—and the ongoing instabilities in the financial sector.

All this leads to the need for a concrete investigation of the contingencies of capitalist restructuring in economic crises. Do capitalist states have the institutional capacity—or can they develop the capacity—to prevent financial volatility from undermining capital accumulation? Will the North American working classes passively absorb the costs of the crisis, or build a new platform for resistance that can potentially block and challenge the resolution of the crisis on neoliberal terms? It is to answering these necessarily political questions, so much related to understanding the particular contexts in which crises emerge, that we now turn to analyzing the crisis as it evolved in American capitalism.

CHAPTER THREE

FINANCE, REGULATION, AND THE AMERICAN STATE

"They say they won't intervene. But they will." With these words, Robert Rubin, Bill Clinton's Treasury Secretary, responded to Paul O'Neill, who when he became the first Treasury Secretary under George W. Bush, had openly criticized his predecessor's interventions in the face of what Rubin called "the messy reality of global financial crises."[28] The dramatic combination of financial crisis and state intervention since the summer of 2007 proved Rubin more correct than he could have imagined. But it also demonstrated why those, whether from the Right or the Left, who have only understood the era of neoliberalism ideologically—i.e. in terms of an ideological determination to free markets from states—have had such a weak handle on discerning what really has been going on over the past quarter century.

The era of neoliberalism has been one long history of financial volatility, with the American state leading the world's states in intervening in a series of financial crises. Almost as soon as he was appointed as head of the Federal Reserve, Alan Greenspan immediately dropped buckets of liquidity on Wall Street in response to the 1987 stock market crash. In the wake of the Savings and Loan crisis, the public Resolution Trust Corporation was established in 1989 to buy up bad real estate debt. In Clinton's first term, Wall Street was saved from the consequences of bond defaults during the 1995 Mexican financial crisis by Rubin's use of the Stabilization Exchange Fund. (This Treasury kitty, established during the 1930s, has once again been called into service in the recent crisis.)

During the Asian crisis two years later, Rubin and his Under-Secretary Larry Summers flew to Seoul to dictate the terms of the IMF loan to the South Korean government. And in 1998 (not long after the Japanese government nationalized one of the world's biggest banks), the head of the New York Federal Reserve summoned the CEOs of Wall Street's leading financial firms and told them they would not be allowed to leave the room until they agreed to take over the insolvent hedge fund, Long-Term Capital Management. These quick interventions by the Fed and Treasury, most of them without waiting upon Congressional pressures or approval, showed they were aware of the disastrous consequences that the failure to act quickly to contain each crisis could have on both the domestic and global financial system.

The financial crisis that began in 2007 spawned a series of interventions by the U.S. Treasury and Federal Reserve over the course of the following year as the scale and scope of the crisis became more and more clear. Finally, amidst a dramatic series of bankruptcies and takeovers during the course of a week in September 2008, the U.S. government undertook to buy virtually all the illiquid assets on the balance sheets of financial institutions in the U.S., including those of foreign-owned firms. The Fed and Treasury needed to act not only as lender of last resort, but also, by taking responsibility for buying and trying to sell all those securities that couldn't find a value or market in the current crisis, as *market maker of last resort.*[29] We now know that Federal Reserve Chairman Ben Bernanke had warned Treasury Secretary Hank Paulson the year before that this might be necessary, and Paulson had agreed. "I knew he was right theoretically," he said. "But I also had, and we both did, some hope that, with all the liquidity out there from investors, that after a certain decline that we would reach a bottom."[30] Yet the private market has no secure bottom without the use of state power.

The fundamental relationship between capitalist states and financial markets cannot be understood in terms of how much or little regulation the former puts upon the latter. It needs to be understood in terms of the guarantees the state provides to property, as measured above all in the promise not to default on its bonds—which are themselves the foundation of financial markets' role in capital accumulation. But not all states are equally able, or trusted as willing (especially since the Russian Revolution), to honor these guarantees. The American state came to act in the second half of the 20th century as an entirely new kind of imperial state precisely because it took utmost responsibility for honoring these guarantees itself, while promoting a world order of independent nation states which the new empire would expect to behave as capitalist states, and would discipline accordingly.

A Century of Crises

It might be thought that the exposure of the state's role in the recent financial crisis would once and for all rid people of the illusion that capitalists don't want their states involved in their markets, or that capitalist states could ever be neutral and benign regulators in the public interest of markets. Unfortunately, the widespread call today for the American state to "go back" to playing the role of such a regulator reveals that this illusion remains deeply engrained, and obscures an understanding of both the past and present history of the relationship between the state and finance in the U.S.

In October 1907, near the beginning of the "American Century," and exactly a hundred years before the onset of the recent financial crisis, the U.S. experienced a financial crisis that for anyone living through it would have seemed as great. Indeed, there were far more suicides in that crisis, as "Wall Street spent a cliff-hanging year" which spanned a stock market crash, an 11 percent decline in GDP, and accelerating runs on the banks.[31] At the core of the crisis was the practice of trust companies drawing money from banks at exorbitant interest rates and, without the protection of sufficient cash reserves, lending out so much of it against stock and bond speculation, so that almost half of the bank loans in New York had questionable securities as their only collateral. When the trust companies were forced to call in some of their loans to stock market speculators, even interest rates which zoomed to well over 100 percent on margin loans could not attract funds. European investors started withdrawing funds from the U.S.

Whereas European central banking had its roots in "haute finance" far removed from the popular classes, U.S. small farmers' dependence on credit had made them hostile to a central bank that they recognized would serve bankers' interests. In the absence of a central bank, both the U.S. Treasury and Wall Street relied on JP Morgan to organize the bail out of 1907. As Henry Paulson did with Lehman's a century later, Morgan let the giant Knickerbocker Trust go under in spite of its holding $50 million of deposits for 17,000 depositors ("I've got to stop somewhere," Morgan said). This only fuelled the panic and triggered runs on other financial firms including the Trust Company of America (leading Morgan to pronounce that "this is the place to stop the trouble"). Using $25 million put at his disposal by the Treasury, and calling together Wall Street's bank presidents to demand they put up another $25 million "within ten or twelve minutes" (which they did), Morgan dispensed the liquidity that began to calm the markets.[32]

When the Federal Reserve was finally established in 1913, this was seen as Woodrow Wilson's great victory over the unaccountable big financiers. As Chernow's monumental biography of Morgan put it, "From the ashes of 1907 arose the Federal Reserve System: everyone saw that thrilling rescues by corpulent old tycoons were a tenuous prop for the banking system."[33] Yet the main elements of the Federal Reserve Bill had already been drafted by the Morgan and Rockefeller interests during the previous Taft administration; and although the Fed's corporatist and decentralized structure of regional federal reserve boards reflected the compromise the final Act made with populist pressures, its immediate effect was actually to cement the "fusion of financial and government power."[34]

This was so both in the sense of the Fed's remit as the "banker's bank"—that is, a largely passive regulator of bank credit and a lender of last resort—and also by virtue of the close ties between the Federal Reserve Bank of New York and the House of Morgan. William McAdoo, Wilson's Treasury Secretary, saw the Federal Reserve Act's provisions allowing U.S. banks to establish foreign branches in terms of laying the basis for the U.S. "to become the dominant financial power of the world and to extend our trade to every part of the world."[35]

In fact, in its early decades, the Fed actually was "a loose and inexperienced body with minimal effectiveness even in its domestic functions."[36] This was an important factor in the crash of 1929 and in the Fed's perverse role in contributing to the Great Depression. It was class pressures from below that produced FDR's union and welfare reforms, but the New Deal is misunderstood if it is simply seen in terms of a dichotomy of purpose and function between state and capitalist actors. While the Morgan empire was brought low by an alliance of new financial competitors and the state, the New Deal's financial reforms, which were introduced before the union and welfare ones, protected the banks as a whole from hostile popular sentiments.

The New Deal regulatory structure restrained competition and excesses of speculation, not so much by curbing the power of finance, but rather through the fortification of key financial institutions via a corporatist "network of public and semi-public bodies, individual firms and professional groups" that existed in a symbiotic relationship with one another distanced from democratic pressures.[37] It oversaw fixed interest rate ceilings and brokerage fees and the new boundaries established between commercial and investment banks, on which basis the New York investment banks were to grow ever more powerful.

Despite the hostility of capitalists to FDR's union and welfare reforms, by the time World War II began the New Dealers had struck what they themselves called their 'grand truce' with business.[38] And even though the Treasury's Keynesian economists raised the hackles of a resilient U.S. financial capital by taking the lead in rewriting the rules of international finance during World War II, Wall Street was by no means external to the constitution of the new international regulatory order established at the conference in Bretton Woods, New Hampshire in 1944. Wall Street was embedded within that order and determined the particular character of this international agreement that established a fixed system of exchange rates to the dollar (and the dollar's exchange rate to gold) and set up the IMF and World Bank and the overall framework of policies for managing states' balance of payments problems.

Markets, States and American Empire

Since World War II the American state has been not just the dominant state in the capitalist world, but the state responsible for overseeing the expansion of capitalism to its current global dimensions and for organizing the management of its economic contradictions. The American state has done this not by displacing other states, but rather by penetrating and integrating them into its orbit. This included the internationalization of these states in the sense of gaining their cooperation in taking responsibility for global accumulation within their borders and their cooperation in setting the international rules for trade and investment.

It was the credibility of the American state's guarantees to property which ensured that, even amidst the Great Depression and business hostility to the New Deal's union and welfare reforms, private funds were readily available as loans to all the new public agencies created in that era. This was also why whatever liquid foreign funds could escape the capital controls of other states in that decade made their way to New York and why so much of the world's gold filled the vaults of Fort Knox. As New York became the world's financial centre and the American state the world's creditor, it also moved to become the guarantor of capitalist banking as well.

This helps explain why the American state took responsibility for making international capitalism viable again after 1945. With the fixed exchange rate of the dollar to gold established at Bretton Woods, the U.S. currency effectively became the global currency, and fundamental store and measure of value in the international arena. When it proved by the 1960s that those who held U.S. dollars would have to suffer a devaluation of their funds through inflation, the fiction of a continuing gold standard was abandoned. The world's financial system was now explicitly based on the dollar as American-made "fiat money," backed by an iron clad guarantee against default of U.S. Treasury bonds, which were now treated as "good as gold."

In the post war period, the New Deal regulatory structure acted as an incubator for financial capital's growth and development. The strong position of Wall Street was institutionally crystallized via the 1951 Accord reached between the Federal Reserve and the Treasury, which was designed to ensure that "forces seen as more radical" within any administration would find it difficult, at least without creating a crisis, to implement inflationary monetary policies.[39] The Fed now stopped making Treasury bonds available only at a fixed price but joined with investment banks in creating a market in these bonds whereby dealers could take speculative positions and thus allow "market forces" to determine Treasury bond prices.[40] Bond traders could thus increase the cost of running government deficits, and this allayed Wall Street's lingering concerns that Keynesian commitments to the priority of full employment and fiscal deficits might prevail in the Treasury.

In the 1950s, profits in the financial sector were already growing faster than in industry. By the early 1960s, the securitization of commercial banking (selling saving certificates rather than relying on deposits) and the enormous expansion of investment banking (including Morgan Stanley's creation of the first viable computer model for analyzing financial risk) were already in train. With the development of the unregulated Euromarket in dollars and the international expansion of U.S. multinational corporations, the playing field for American finance was far larger than New Deal regulations could contain.

Both domestically and internationally, the baby had outgrown the incubator, which was in any case being buffeted by inflationary pressures stemming from union militancy and public expenditures on the Great Society programs and the Vietnam War. The bank crisis of 1966, the rise of pension funds which complained about non-competitive brokerage fees protected by New Deal regulations, the series of scandals that beset Wall Street by the end of the decade—all this foretold the end of the corporatist structure of brokers, investment banks and corporate managers that had dominated domestic capital markets since the New Deal, culminating in Wall Street's "Big Bang" of 1975.

Meanwhile, the Bretton Woods fixed exchange rate system collapsed by the early 1970s, due to inflationary pressures on the dollar as well as the massive growth in international trade and investment. With a dollar no longer nominally tied to gold, those who held U.S. assets had to live with the fluctuating value of the U.S. dollar. This laid the foundation for the derivatives revolution by leading to a massive demand for hedging risk to offset the dollar's oscillations by trading futures and options in exchange and interest rates. The Commodity Futures Trading Commission was created in 1974 less to regulate this new market than to facilitate its development.[41] It was not so much neoliberal ideology that broke the New Deal system of financial regulations as it was the contradictions that had emerged within that system.

If there was going to be any serious alternative to giving financial capital its head by the 1970s, this would have required going well beyond the old regulations and capital controls, and introducing qualitatively new policies to undermine rather than protect the social power of finance. This was recognized in the U.S. by those pushing for the more radical aspects of the 1977 Community Reinvestment Act, who could have never foretold where the compromises struck with the banks to secure their loans would lead. The CRA, which was the main legislative victory for the Left of the Democratic Party during the Carter Administration, required commercial banks to allocate 5 percent of their working capital for home and small business loans in poor communities. It was passed in the teeth of opposition from the banks, yet it in fact did little for local economic development. It ultimately contributed to the great housing collapse and financial breakdown of 2007 via the concession offered to the banks that the government sponsored mortgage companies, Freddie Mac and Fannie Mae, would encourage the secondary mortgage securities market to relieve the burden of banks being required to make loans to poor people.

Where socialist politics were stronger, the nationalization of the financial system was being forcefully advanced as a demand by the mid 1970s. The Left in the British Labour Party was able to secure the passage of a conference resolution to nationalize the big banks and insurance companies in the City of London, albeit with no effect on a Labour Government that embraced one of the IMF's first structural adjustment programs. In France, the *Programme Commun* of the 1970s led to the Mitterrand Government's bank nationalizations at the beginning of the 1980s, but this was carried through in a way that ensured that the structure and function of the banks were not changed in the process. In Canada, directly elected local planning boards, which would draw on the surplus from a nationalized financial system to create jobs, were proposed by the Left as the first step in a new strategy to get labor movements to think in ways that were not so cramped and defensive.[42]

Such alternatives—strongly opposed even by social democratic politicians who soon accommodated themselves to the dynamics of finance-led neoliberalism and the ideology of efficient free markets—were soon forgotten amidst the general defeat of labor movements and socialist politics that characterized the new era. Financial capitalists took the lead in demanding the defeat of those domestic social forces they blamed for creating the inflationary pressures which undermined the value of their assets. The further growth of financial markets, increasingly characterized by competition, innovation and flexibility, was central to the resolution of the crisis of the 1970s.

Neoliberalism and the New Age of Finance

Perhaps the most important aspect of the new age of finance was the central role it played in disciplining and integrating labor into markets as workers, consumers, savers and home-owners. The industrial and political pressures from below that characterized the crisis of the 1970s could not have been countered and defeated without the discipline that a financial order built upon the mobility of capital placed upon firms. Shareholder value was in many respects a euphemism for how the discipline imposed by the competition for global investment funds was transferred to the high wage proletariat of the advanced capitalist countries. New York and London's access to global savings simultaneously came to depend on the surplus extracted through the high rates of exploitation of the new working classes in "emerging markets."

At the same time, the very constraints that the mobility of capital had on working class incomes in the rich countries had the effect of further integrating these workers into the realm of finance. This was most obvious in terms of their increasing debt loads amidst the universalization of the credit card. But it also pertained to how workers grew more attuned to financial markets, as they followed the stock exchanges and mutual funds that their pension funds were invested in, often cheered by rising stocks as firms were restructured without much thought to the layoffs involved.

Both the explosion of finance and the disciplining of labor were a necessary condition for the dramatic productive transformations in this era. The leading role that finance came to play over the past three decades, including the financialization of industrial corporations and the greatest growth in profits taking place in the financial sector, has often been viewed as undermining production and representing little else than speculation and a source of unsustainable bubbles. But this fails to account for why this era—a period that was longer in duration than the "golden age"—lasted so long.

In fact, the era between the crisis of the 1970s and the outbreak of the current crisis has been one of capitalist dynamism, including significant technological revolutions, involving not just the deepening and expansion of capital, but also the radical restructuring of corporations and firms and indeed of capitalist social relations and culture in general. This was especially the case for the U.S. itself, where financial competition, innovation, flexibility *and* volatility accompanied the reconstitution of the American material base at home and its expansion abroad. Overall, the era of finance-led neoliberalism experienced a rate of growth of global GDP that compares favorably with earlier periods of capitalist development over the last two centuries.[43]

It is, in any case, impossible to imagine the globalization of capitalist production without the type of financial intermediation in the circuits of capital imparted by derivatives and other financial instruments that help offset the risks associated with flexible exchange rates, interest rates variations across national borders, uncertain transportation and commodity costs, etc. Moreover, as competition to access more mobile finance intensified, this imposed discipline on firms (and states) which forced restructuring within firms and reallocated capital across sectors. This included the provision of venture capital to the new information and bio-medical sectors which have become leading arenas of accumulation.

At the same time, the U.S. investment banks spread their tentacles abroad for three decades through their global role in corporate mergers and acquisitions and Initial Public Offerings of corporate stock. During the course of this relationships between finance and production, including their legal and accounting frameworks, were radically changed around the world in ways that increasingly resembled American patterns. This was reinforced by the bilateral and multilateral international trade and investment treaties (pioneered by the Canada–U.S. Free Trade Agreement and its successor NAFTA) which were increasingly concerned with opening up other economies to New York's and London's financial, legal and accounting services.

The commitment by the Federal Reserve—via the high interest rates of the "Volcker shock" of 1979 to 1982—to anti-inflation policies at the expense of stable employment was designed to guarantee the value of Treasury bills as the global store of value. This was a defining moment of U.S. state intervention precisely because of its implications in terms of the class and power relations that have characterized the neoliberal era. Like the current moment, it started in the run-up to a presidential election—that is, *before* Reagan's election—with bipartisan Congressional support and industrial capital backing the new leading role this marked for financial capital in the U.S. and abroad. As the American state took the initiative, by its example and its pressure on other states around the world, to give priority to low inflation as a much stronger and ongoing commitment than before, this bolstered finance capital's confidence in the substantive value of lending; and after the initial astronomical interest rates produced by the Volcker shock, this soon made an era of low interest rates possible.

Throughout the neoliberal era, the enormous demand for U.S. bonds and the low interest paid on them has rested on the confidence the Volcker shock gave to financial markets everywhere that the Fed and Treasury were committed above all to an anti-inflation policy priority as part and parcel of guaranteeing the value of U.S. bonds. This was reinforced by the defeat of American trade unionism in the early 1980s, highlighted first by the concessions forced on the UAW as part of the conditions the Carter administration imposed on Chrysler in saving it from bankruptcy, and then by Reagan's deliberate breaking of the Air Traffic Controllers' union. But it was also a product of the intense competition in financial markets domestically and internationally. This played itself out in terms of financial capital putting pressure on firms to lower costs through restructuring in order to access financial markets, as well as reallocating capital across sectors, especially through venture funds to support new technologies. The "Americanization of finance" in other states, involving U.S. banks increasingly operating directly abroad and domestic banks competing with them by emulating their practices, also played a important corollary role in the flow of global savings from the early 1980s to the U.S. economy.

Deregulation was more a consequence than the main cause of the intense competition in financial markets and its attendant effects. By 1990, this competition had already led to banks scheming to escape the reserve requirements of the Basel bank regulations by creating Structured Investment Vehicles to hold these and other risky derivative assets. It also led to the increased blurring of the lines between commercial and investment banking, insurance and the real estate sector of the U.S. economy. Competition in the financial sector fostered all kinds of new instruments which allowed for high leveraging (i.e. increasing the ratio of loans to bank reserves) of the funds that could be accessed via low interest rates. This meant that there was an explosion in credit and the effective money supply. (This was highly ironic in terms of the monetarist theories that are usually thought to have founded neoliberalism, whose talisman was limiting the growth in money supply as the foundation for economic stability.)

The competition to purchase assets with these funds replaced price inflation with the asset inflation that characterized the whole era. This was reinforced by the American state's readiness to throw further liquidity into the financial system whenever a specific asset bubble burst—while imposing austerity on economies in the Global South as the condition for the liquidity the IMF and World Bank provided to their financial markets at moments of crisis. All this was central to the uneven and often chaotic making of global capitalism over the past quarter century, to the crises that have punctuated it, and to the active role of the U.S. state in containing them. Meanwhile, the world beat a path to U.S. financial markets not only because of the demand for Treasury bills, and not only because of Wall Street's linkages to U.S. capital more generally, but also because of the depth and breadth of those financial markets.

Financing the American Dream: From "Great Society" to "Subprime Society"

The American Dream has always materially entailed promoting the integration of the popular classes into the circuits of financial capital, whether as independent commodity farmers, as workers whose pay checks were deposited with banks and whose pension savings were invested in the stock market, as consumers reliant on credit, and not least as heavily mortgaged home owners. This incorporation of the mass of the American population was as or more important to the dynamism and longevity of the finance-led neoliberal era than the degree of supposed deregulation of financial markets. But it also helped trigger the current crisis—and the massive state intervention in response to it.

The scale of the current crisis, which significantly has its roots in housing finance, cannot be understood apart from how the defeat of American trade unionism since the early 1980s played out by the first years of the 21st century. In spite of stagnating wages and growing class inequality, this defeat did not bring about an absolute deterioration of living standards for most American working families. This is because high levels of consumption, including on increasingly expensive health care, were sustained by the lower prices of consumer goods produced by cheap labor abroad, by the accumulation of household debt rather than saving, and by the intensification of family labor—more family members working longer hours under more severe working conditions.

Constrained in what they could get from their labor for two decades, and dependent on debt for consumption, working class families were drawn, however, into the logic of asset inflation not only through the institutional investment of their pensions, but also through the one major asset they held in their own hands (or could aspire to hold)— their family home. It was the inegalitarian effects of neoliberal policies that pushed Americans to base many of their financial decisions on the belief, amply encouraged by both the private and public institutions enmeshed in the U.S. financial system, that home ownership was risk-free and guaranteed annual increases in equity.

It is significant that this included the attempted integration via financial markets of poor African-American communities, so long the Achilles heel of working class integration into the mythology of the American Dream. As the "Great Society" public expenditure programs of the 1960s ran up against the need to redeem the imperial state's anti-inflationary commitments, financial markets became the mechanism for doing this. One of the great ironies of the legacy of the civil rights and feminist movements was that as banks and credit card companies were pressed to develop color and gender blind risk models—creating greater opportunity for more and more people to become debtors (with higher interest rates, of course, for those with lower incomes)—they also subjected more and more people to the patterns of discipline, subordination and crisis within contemporary financial markets.

From the 1980s, amidst the Reagan administration's assault on labor rights and public services, the practice began whereby home-owners tried to take advantage of the "wealth effect" of rising home values by using that as collateral to taking on more debt. The reorganization of the mortgage sector in the wake of the Savings and Loans crisis, including through the increased bundling and selling on of mortgages as securities, fostered the link between consumption and real estate values. This combined with the allure of homeownership to create a self-reinforcing spiral of growing market demand and rising home prices. The Clinton administration especially sought to integrate working-class Black and Hispanic communities into mainstream housing markets through its promotion of wider access to financial services and market-based alternatives to public housing and income supports in order to "end welfare as we know it."

By the end of the decade, such unsettling events as the Asian financial crisis and the collapse of the dot-com boom increased the risk of investments in the stock market, whether directly or through pension funds. In this context, the housing market emerged as a key source of wealth for many American wage earners, embodying the one significant asset they could actually hope to possess. All these developments served both to extend the reach of financial relations and to establish the growth of household debt as a key anchor of American financial growth.

Of course, the desire to realize the American Dream of home ownership on the part of so many of those who had previously been excluded was one thing; actual access to residential markets was another. They could only do so in such unprecedented numbers by the turn of the century because financial intermediaries were frantically creating domestic mortgage debt in order to package and resell it in the market for structured credit. Already well under way during the 1990s, the trend was given a great fillip by the Bush administration's determination to open up competition to sell and trade mortgage-related securities as well as by the Fed's lowering of real interest rates in the aftermath of the dot-com meltdown and 9/11.

With most strata of middle income earners already in the market, mortgage companies structured loans in such a way as to capture consumers who could not otherwise have afforded home ownership. The majority of these loans were Adjustable Rate Mortgages (ARMs) with initial two-year fixed-rate periods at lower interest rates. In addition, a growing number of mortgage providers offered debtors the option of limiting their monthly payments to the interest or even less, so that the principal would increase over time. By 2006 subprime loans represented 28 percent of total U.S. mortgages, and subprime mortgage-backed securities had become the largest component of the American market for asset-backed securities, accounting for nearly half of all issues.[44]

Commercial banks competed to extend residential mortgages to anyone breathing and then combined these mortgages into new "derivative" securities which they sold on to other financial intermediaries (including the Special Investment Vehicles they used to create the shadow banking system) as well as to the government sponsored mortgage corporations Fannie Mae and Freddie Mac. The possibility of earning fees on debts that could be moved off their balance sheet made banks more willing to increase their exposure to low-income households, knowing very well the risks were greater they would not be able to pay their debts as interest rates rose.

Between 2000 and 2006 house prices rose faster than during any other period in recent U.S. history, with medium real home prices growing from $169,428 to $276,324.[45] The bubble in mortgage finance that emerged inside the U.S. housing sector was supported and reinforced by the tendency among developing economies, above all China, to peg their currencies to the dollar and to recycle their growing export earnings into the American market, including mortgages. But even beyond this, private capital flowed from around the world to the nodes of the global circuit of capital located in the U.S. This raised asset prices, lowered interest rates, and intensified competitive pressures on investors to procure higher yields through greater leveraging and innovative securitization to stretch the boundaries of risk.

Encouraged by rising home prices and by mortgage tax deductions, growing segments of the home-owning working class sustained their consumption as wages stagnated by taking out second mortgages on the bubble-inflated values of their homes. The acceleration of mortgage-backed securitization, taking place amidst rising house prices that seemed to increase the wealth and creditworthiness of those borrowing, gave rise to the acceptance of lower standards by regulatory agencies, acting with the connivance of both parties in Congress. The Republicans' determination to open up competition to sell and trade mortgages and mortgage-backed securities to all comers was in turn reinforced by the Greenspan Fed's dramatic lowering of real interest to almost zero in response to the bursting of the dot-com bubble and to 9/11. But this was a policy that was only sustainable via the flow of global savings to the U.S., not least to the apparent Treasury-plated safety of Fannie Mae and Freddie Mac securities as government sponsored enterprises.

Much of this edifice of financial obligations was built through the shadow banking system which did not fall under the Federal Reserve's regulatory purview and therefore were not subject to constraining rules such as reserve requirements. The shadow banking system opened up to a wider world of structured finance, where mathematical wizards used complex models to build "nested structures of Russian dolls"[46]—a complex and opaque world of asset-backed securities, derivative instruments based on those, more derivatives based in turn on those derivatives, and an infinite variety of insurance instruments (mostly credit default swaps). It was thus a long chain of neoliberal connections that led to the massive funding of mortgages, the hedging and default derivatives based on this, their treatment as AAA low risk safe investments by bond rating agencies such as Moody's, and their spread onto the books of many foreign institutions.

The great New York investment banks, whose traditional business was corporate and government finance, were themselves fully involved in buying and selling the derivatives based on mortgages sold in poor communities in the U.S. and then repackaged and resold many times over. It also included the world's biggest insurance company, AIG, which had made a massive business out of selling under-funded insurance on these derivatives even while subject to the highly regulated insurance regime in the U.S. The worlds of high and low finance had never been so closely interconnected than in this volatile mix of global capital movements, insecurity and poverty.

The Federal Reserve emphatically made the case that "information processing technologies [had] enabled creditors to achieve significant efficiencies in collecting and assimilating the data necessary to evaluate risk;"[47] and it increasingly defined its role as that of promoting financial education for the masses. "Like all learning," as Greenspan put it, "financial education is a process that should begin at an early age and last throughout life."[48] It certainly got people to think of themselves as investors by thinking of family homes as an asset. But neoliberalism never delivered on its promise of a hidden hand equilibrating financial markets alongside a mass public of informed, financially literate borrowers and investors.

This was borne out by the sale of derivatives around the world based on mortgages whose risk was scarcely evaluated at all. And it was borne out by the success that mortgage brokers had in manipulating people into taking out expensive loans by using a variety of techniques—teaser rate, adjustable rates, hiding the real terms in the small print, among others—designed to confuse borrowers as to the real cost of their loan, as well as the fact that many subprime loans with frightening interest rates went to households that would have easily qualified for a regular mortgage loan with less exploitative terms. Securitization techniques as they had evolved over the past decade produced tremendous pressure on, or temptation for, brokers to pursue ever more aggressive sales strategies. Predatory lending was not eradicated; rather, it went mainstream.

Had the Federal Reserve and the Treasury been so inclined, they certainly could have made considerably more efforts to impose some regulations (or to get other regulators to do so) to limit the banks' practices. But their own structural ties to the markets meant that there was not much they were inclined to do. Their authority over the financial system had largely been based on their capacity to steer markets already strongly biased in favor of expansion. Insofar as they came to be headed by the turn of the century by men like Greenspan with a near-religious faith in the virtues of capitalism—as a follower of Ayn Rand, as close as it gets to a capitalist religion—was probably more symptom than cause.

CHAPTER FOUR

CRISIS MANAGEMENT FROM BUSH TO OBAMA

In his 2003 memoir, Robert Rubin claims that his experience at Goldman Sachs had taught him that there were "situations where derivatives put additional pressure on volatile markets" and that "many people who used derivatives didn't fully understand the risks they were taking," but that Larry Summers, his deputy at the Treasury "thought I was overly concerned with the risk of derivatives."[49] It was the latter view that prevailed when, with Summers having succeeded Rubin as Treasury Secretary, the Commodity Futures Modernization Act was passed in the dying months of the Clinton Administration. After Bush's election, Rubin went back to Wall Street (moving from Goldman Sachs to Citibank), while Summers relocated to the presidency of Harvard, which seemed to suggest a greater independence from financial capital. Summers' appointment as Senior Economic Advisor to the Obama Administration was thus an apparent contrast to the pipeline that seemed to link Wall Street, and especially Goldman Sachs, to the Treasury and the White House under both the Clinton and later Bush Administrations. Nevertheless, on April 4, 2009 the *Washington Post* disclosed that in 2008 Summers had "collected roughly $5.2 million in compensation from hedge fund D. E. Shaw" as well as over "$2.7 million in speaking fees from several troubled Wall Street firms and other organizations."[50]

What could clearly be seen at work here was the complex intertwining of public and private careers and interests that informed the relationship between state and market institutions, especially those that linked Wall Street with Washington, D.C. In the absence of a traditional bureaucracy in the American state, leading corporate lawyers and financiers have moved between Wall Street and Washington ever since the age of the "robber barons" in the late 19th century. Taking time off from the private firm to engage in public service has been called the "institutional schizophrenia" that links these Wall Street figures as "double agents" to the state. While acting in one sphere to squeeze through every regulatory loophole, they act in the other to introduce new regulations as "a tool for the efficient management of the social order in the public interest."[51] Not to mention the thousands of lower level links, this defined the role played by individuals like McChesney Martin and Douglas Dillon in the Eisenhower and Kennedy administrations no less than that of Robert Rubin and Hank Paulson in the Clinton and Bush administrations.

It is partly for this reason that the long history of popular protest and discontent triggered by financial scandals and crises in the U.S., far from undermining the institutional and regulatory basis of financial expansion, have repeatedly been pacified through the processes of further "codification, institutionalization, and juridification," as rules became more elaborate, as the regulatory institutions applying them acquired more resources, and as the courts were increasingly involved in interpreting them.[52] And far from buckling under the pressure of popular disapproval, financial elites have proved very adept at not only responding to these pressures but also using them to create new regulatory frameworks that have laid the foundations for the further growth of financial capital, including in terms of class and institutional power. The capital adequacy rules that states adopted for banks from the 1980s onwards had precisely the effect.

Nor is this a matter of simple manipulation of the masses. Most people have an interest, however contradictory, in the daily functioning and reproduction of financial capitalism because of their dependence on it: from access to their wages and salaries via their bank accounts, to buying goods and services on credit, to paying their bills, to investing their savings. They depend on it, moreover, for the very roofs over their heads let alone the investment in their homes as assets for retirement. So much was this the case that by the first decade of the

21st century, American capitalism was enveloped in a financial system premised on a massive funding of mortgages and consumer credit. And this was facilitated by the jumble of derivative and securitized instruments which, once wrapped in the triple-A status bequeathed by the rating agencies, could be spread onto the books of a wide variety of financial institutions both at home and abroad.

Triggering the Crisis

When a housing bubble bursts it affects not just the financial system, but the whole economic system in a way stock market meltdowns do not. This is so because of the way housing bridges finance and the rest of the economy—most directly the construction industry as well as furniture and appliances. Since for most people the value of the family home accounts for most of their wealth by far, any significant decline in that value can undermine consumer confidence.

To understand how the crisis was triggered it is necessary to pick up here from the last chapter's discussion on housing finance. The housing boom had reached its peak by the end of 2004 and began to really weaken in the second half of 2005, when inventories of unsold homes jumped up and house prices began to decline. The problems in the residential mortgage market can be traced directly to households' growing mortgage payment burdens. In the short term, Americans were able to manage this burden by (re)financing at attractive interest rates and cashing in the equity in their homes. But this of course only added to the structural burden. Meanwhile, as families pressed against the limits of continually increasing their total working hours, the real income of the median U.S. household fell between 1999 and 2005.[53] In 2005, when the teaser period of ultra low interest rates began to end (in some cases, rates on subprime mortgages doubled or even trebled), the average national variable mortgage rate jumped from 5.3 percent to 6.2 percent.[54] During the same period, the Fed (once again feeling the need to offer inflation-proof guarantees as the world's central banker) decided to step on the brakes and raised the federal funds rate by a full four percentage points between mid-2004 and mid-2006. This translated into even higher interest premiums on subprime issues. By 2006, the delinquency rate on subprime mortgages rose by 4.4 percent, in 2007, by 16.7 percent.[55]

On the eve of the crisis, subprime residential mortgage-backed securities and mortgage-linked collateralized debt obligations still comprised 60 percent of the American market for asset-backed securities. The dramatic growth of securitized subprime mortgages meant that the whole financial system had become extremely vulnerable to the volatility in this segment of the market. Select investors began to view the market as inflated and to back away from mortgage-backed securities. As it became clear that the growth of this market was largely dependent on the continued entry of low-income borrowers and that the default rate of non-prime borrowers vastly exceeded actuarial projections, the value of structured instruments came under pressure and their supply slowed down. From 2006 to 2007 the issuance of asset-backed securities slumped by 29.4 percent, led by a 69.1 percent collapse in the new supply of collateralized debt obligations and subprime mortgage-backed securities.[56]

Since the expansion of securitized mortgage debt had taken place through the construction of complex chains of interconnected financial networks, the malaise in the mortgage market spread quickly to other sectors. The globalized nature of American finance meant that foreign investors who were major players in the U.S. markets took immediate losses. The collapse of the U.S. housing bubble was also spread internationally because of the complex ways that collateralized mortgages are constructed, with the result that broad segments of the financial sectors in Europe as well as North America were quickly drawn into the collapse of non-prime risk. Moreover, since the spreading of risk in subprime mortgages had been effected through their packaging in derivatives with more secure forms of debt, the subprime crisis undermined the econometric equations that valued these assets in global markets. Mortgage-backed securities held so broadly by financial institutions around the world now became difficult to value and to sell and this produced a contagion throughout securitized financial and inter-bank markets.

From Dream to Nightmare I: Crisis Management under Bush

As the financial crisis broke out in the summer of 2007, the newly appointed Chairman of the Fed, Ben Bernanke, could draw on his academic work as an economist at Princeton University on how the 1929 crash could have been prevented,[57] and Treasury Secretary Henry Paulson could draw on his own illustrious career (like Rubin's) as a senior executive at Goldman Sachs. Both the Treasury and Federal Reserve staff worked closely with the Securities Exchange Commission and Commodity Futures Trading Commission under the rubric of the President's Working Group on Financial Markets that had been set up in 1988 and known on Wall Street as the "Plunge Protection Team."

During the summer of 2007, it was widely reported that large amounts of debt were owed by U.S. households that were simply incapable of generating the income streams needed for their repayment. In an era when few data are not recorded and analyzed, banks had ended up holding assets that they were unable to value. For once a debt had been "securitized"—that is, sliced up, mixed with a variety of other debts, and then sold as a new composite asset-backed security—there was little hope of tracing in any meaningful way the value of the resulting new "asset." Former Treasury Secretary Paul O'Neill summarized the nature of the problem facing debt markets in this way: "If you had ten bottles of water and one bottle had poison in it, and you didn't know which one, you probably wouldn't drink any one."[58]

Over the ensuing months, the U.S. Treasury organized, first, a consortium of international banks and investment funds and then an overlapping consortium of mortgage companies, financial securitizers and investment funds, to take concrete measures to calm the markets. As it had done a decade earlier during the Long Term Capital Management crisis, Treasury officials convened the CEOs of the nation's ten largest commercial banks in September 2007.[59] This time, however, the attempt to use the Treasury's authority to get the major banks to act to stabilize the system did not succeed: no one would invest in debt backed by subprime mortgages, which were at the heart of the problem.

For its part, the Federal Reserve acted as the world's central bank by repeatedly supplying other central banks with dollars to provide liquidity to their banking systems, while doing the same for Wall Street. The global attraction and strength of American finance was seen to be rooted in its depth and breadth at home and this meant that when the crisis hit in the subprime security market of the heart of the empire, it immediately had implications for the banking systems of many other countries. The scale of the American government's intervention has certainly been a function of the consequent unraveling of the crisis throughout its integrated domestic financial system, yet it is also important to understand this in terms of the American state's imperial responsibilities in terms of managing the contradictions of global capitalism, and coordinating the responses to the crisis—and the eventual "exit strategies" out of the crisis—of finance ministries and central banks.

This is why the Fed repeatedly pumped billions of dollars via foreign central banks into inter-bank markets abroad, where banks balance their books through the overnight borrowing of dollars from other banks. An important factor in the nationalizations of Fannie Mae and Freddie Mac was the need to ratify the expectations of foreign investors, including the Japanese and Chinese central banks, who had invested in the securities of these "government sponsored enterprises" that the U.S. government would never default on its debt obligations. It is for this reason that even those foreign leaders who have opportunistically pronounced the end of American 'financial superpower status' have credited the U.S. Treasury for "acting not just in the U.S. interests but also in the interests of other nations."[60]

The U.S. was not being altruistic in doing this, since not to do it would have risked a run on the dollar. But this is precisely the point. The American state cannot act in the interests of American capitalism without also reflecting the logic of American capitalism's integration with global capitalism both economically and politically. This is why it is always misleading to portray the American state as merely representing its "national interest" while ignoring the structural role it plays in the making and reproduction of global capitalism.

Both the Treasury and Federal Reserve staff continued to work through the President's Working Group on Financial Markets to facilitate regulatory cooperation and quick policy responses to coordinate their activities with the Securities Exchange Commission and Commodity Futures Trading Commission. As 2008 began with stock markets in Asia and Europe shaken at the prospect of a serious American recession, the Fed undertook a large emergency cut in interest rates. By March it had undertaken another coordinated move with the other central banks, supplying them with dollars to provide liquidity to their banks, while simultaneously making no less than $200 billion available to Wall Street's investment banks. Yet even this could not save all the banks.

The headlines that greeted St. Patrick's Day 2008—"Wall Street Quakes as the Parade Passes By"—revealed that after all day and night weekend sessions the Fed had directed, overseen and guaranteed to the tune of $30 billion JP Morgan's takeover of Bear Stearns. Essentially the Fed had agreed to take full responsibility for the risk associated with low-grade investments. Ironically, Bear Stearns had been the lone major investment bank which had refused to cooperate with the Fed-engineered bailout of Long Term Capital Management a decade before.

The Bear Stearns crisis was somewhat of a watershed, as it made clear to regulators just how deep the cracks in the system ran and how forceful and effective the regulatory response would have to be. By the end of the month, when the Treasury issued its long-awaited "Blueprint for a Modernized Financial Regulatory Structure" (in preparation since March 2007, before the onset of the crisis), it did not just announce plans for the further formalization of coordination of the interventions undertaken by the U.S. and British Treasuries. The blueprint was primarily designed to enhance the Fed's regulatory authority over the whole financial system, not least over the investment banks for whom it now was so openly the lender of last resort. The Fed now placed a staff of analysts inside each of Wall Street's investment banks in order to collect important information.

What had been such a key monetary policy instrument during the Greenspan era—the announcements of marginal charges of the federal funds rate—did not have much leverage in a situation where the inter-bank loans had become almost fully paralyzed by anxiety-driven, liquidity-hoarding behavior. With the Fed rapidly approaching a situation where interest rates could not be lowered any further, it dramatically expanded its programs for helping the banks by "repurchasing agreements" ("repos"), thereby hugely enhancing its capacity to provide liquidity and sector-specific support. Through a related program (the Term Securities Lending Facility) the Fed transferred what was then a stunning $219 billion in risky assets from financial institutions to its own books in the months following the Bear Stearns collapse.

But all of this state intervention, however much it was founded on a legacy of relatively successful efforts to contain crises in the past, could not prevent this crisis from assuming still greater proportions. Although most serious analysts thought the worst was over in the spring, by the summer of 2008 Fannie Mae and Freddie Mac were also being undone by the crisis. By September so were the great New York investment banks. The problem they all faced was that there was no market for a great proportion of the mortgage-backed assets on their books. As financial capital's risk evaluation equations unraveled, so did the ability of financial markets to judge the worth of financial institutions' balance sheets.

Banks became very reluctant to give each other even the shortest-term credits. Without such inter-bank credit, any financial system will collapse. The unprecedented scale of interventions in September 2008 can only be understood in this context. They involved pumping additional hundred of billions of dollars into the world's inter-bank markets; the nationalizations of Fannie Mae, Freddie Mac and AIG; the seizure and fire sale of Washington Mutual to prevent the largest bank failure in U.S. history; a blanket guarantee on the $3.4 trillion in mutual funds deposits; a ban on short-selling of financial stocks; *and* Paulson's $700 billion "Troubled Asset Relief Program" (TARP) to take on toxic mortgage assets.

The takeover of Fannie Mae and Freddie Mac created little additional liquidity in markets for mortgage-backed securities, let alone in those subprime market segments where Freddie and Fannie had no presence. During the following week two major investment banks found themselves heading for disaster. One catastrophe was averted when, through regulatory orchestration, Merrill Lynch was sold to Bank of America, but another was not—the American government's reluctance to extend financial guarantees complicated last-minute efforts to have the old firm of Lehman Brothers bank taken over, with the result that it was forced to file for bankruptcy.

The Fed and Treasury once again convened Wall Street CEOs and urged them to arrange a private sector bailout. But the reluctance to make substantial funds available from the public purse to grease the wheels for this turned out to be a serious miscalculation. Lehman had massive exposure in the markets for securitized products and complex derivatives and its failure sent shockwaves through the markets. In the days and weeks following the bankruptcy, investors questioned the government's capacity to understand the dynamic interconnections in the financial system and its commitment to support its key institutional pillars.

If the government derived one benefit from letting Lehman sink, it was that it lent some credence to the idea that market discipline was not only for ordinary people, but also for Wall Street firms. But it was not permitted to enjoy such new-found ideological coherence for very long. AIG had been forced to write off massive amounts of funds and when the rating agencies downgraded the company's debt they effectively brought it to the brink of insolvency. Its failure would have sent markets around the world in a tailspin, but behind the scenes rescue efforts had already been set in motion and the Federal Reserve quickly made available a sizeable lifeline.

The Federal Reserve had already gone well beyond the normal boundaries of its regulatory remit by extending help to investment banks, and it now ventured into even newer territory as it took responsibility for the survival of an insurance company whose commitments constituted a key pillar of the markets for securitized products and complex derivatives. On the same day that AIG's problems became fully apparent, the price of stock in Reserve Primary, the largest and oldest fund operator in the short-term money market (the safest investments after cash and bank deposits) fell below one dollar. It took the Treasury's insurance of all money market deposits to stabilize the situation.

Even after all this, however, the end to the trouble was nowhere in sight. The Bush government now faced the prospect of becoming involved in an endless series of interventions that would have entangled them in patchworks of ad hoc financial arrangements. In this situation, the Treasury, with Hank Paulson, the former Goldman's CEO at its head, proposed a sweeping plan that, it hoped, would serve to flush sufficient toxic debt out of the system to restore its liquidity. In early October 2008 Congress was finally induced to pass the Economic Stabilization Act, which provided the $700 billion TARP fund to the Treasury.

The Treasury had justified getting these astronomical amounts from Congress in order to save the banks by being able to buy up their toxic assets. In the wake of the markets showing anything but vitality in the following weeks, it exploited the latitude the Act gave it by purchasing equity stakes in financial institutions to provide them with more capital, the mammoth financial conglomerate of Citigroup, above all. Investors began betting against it, sending the share price down more than 60 percent. After having been approached by senior Citigroup officials, regulators at the Federal Reserve, Treasury and the FDIC announced a plan to prop it up.

The fact that the Bush government did not ask for much in return highlighted the contradictions of the Treasury's continued reliance on the "too big to fail" approach. In this crisis, with one firm after another vulnerable to buckling under the weight of their bad investments, the socialization of bankers' losses was increasingly seen to be both ineffective and unfair—a factor that had already played its part in the outcome of the November 2008 election. All this meant, as the U.S. state began accumulating equity stakes, is that for a period it actually owned a very significant part of the nation's financial system. But this had nothing to do with the imposition of effective democratic public control. If the American government was committed to socializing risk, it was not interested in socializing control of the financial system.

From Dream to Nightmare II: Crisis Management under Obama

Obama's appointment of Tim Geithner as his Secretary of the Treasury was predicated on the notion that the central problem he faced was a lack of confidence on Wall Street. As head of the New York Federal Reserve Bank, he was seen as "on-side" with Wall Street, and had been at the epicenter of the Bush government's response to the crisis. Both Geithner and Bernanke (who would be reappointed by Obama as head of the Fed later in 2009) now went out of their way to emphasize that their objective was to keep banks in private hands and that any government control over banks' operations would be strictly temporary. This left it with the same dilemmas and contradictions associated with massive public assistance to a financial sector that was now extremely reluctant to lend in its own self-interest.

The Financial Stability Plan that Geithner unveiled in February and March 2009 to deal with the persistent illiquidity of financial markets followed what had gone before. This was so both in terms of the extended Treasury purchases of bank stock, and the TARF program (the Term Asset-Backed Securities Loan Facility) announced just before the end the previous administration in December 2008. This reached the point of the Fed devoting as much as a trillion dollars to purchasing from the banks the now unmarketable derivatives on their books. And the announced framework for financial sector regulatory reform also followed Paulson's 2007 plan in proposing to expand the supervisory remit of the Fed relative to other agencies to cover all financial institutions posing systemic risk, alongside a financial consumer protection agency and new regulations for the derivatives markets.

One new element, resembling the private-public partnerships that had become so common under neoliberalism, was a plan for five asset management funds to be set up along the lines of the government's

Resolution Trust Corporation during the Savings and Loan crisis. The *Financial Times'* Martin Wolf accurately summed up the essence of the plan: "Under the scheme, the government provides virtually all the finance and bears almost all the risk, but it uses the private sector to price the assets. In return, private investors obtain rewards—perhaps generous rewards—based on their performance via equity participation, alongside the Treasury. I think of this as the 'vulture fund relief scheme'."[61] In the end, this scheme did not have to be used because the scale of the rest of the bailout of the big banks was sufficient to restore their profitability for the most part.

When the Federal Reserve released the results of the "stress test" it had conducted of the nineteen largest U.S. bank holding companies in May 2009 it found that, with the help of government purchase of bank stocks and bad assets, nine of them already had adequate capital. The requirement it put on the others to immediately develop and implement a detailed plan for the regulators to raise additional capital put most of Wall Street's bank in the position to start paying back their loans from the government and buy back their stock. In addition to the direct bailouts, this was accomplished with the help of the profits they were making on the fees they earned marketing government bonds, and on the spread between how cheaply the government made funds available to them and the interest they then charged to their customers as they lent out that money.

The one real innovation of the new administration, not heralded as part of its Financial Stability Plan, was the announcement in March 2009 that the Fed would begin to purchase hundred of billions of dollars of long-term Treasury bonds to help improve conditions in private credit markets. By keeping down the interest costs on its deficit that the government would have to pay, this made more viable its undertaking of the most extensive fiscal stimulus outside of wartime in American history.

This purchasing of government debt by its central bank ("quantitative easing," as it was now called)—and the relative lack of critical comment it induced—was a measure of how shaken the ruling class circles, and the mainstream economists who advise them, were by the severity of the crisis. At almost any time since World War II, anyone suggesting such direct and massive pump-priming would have been judged economically illiterate. A sell-off of Treasuries by other purchasers would have been predicted, amidst a massive run on the dollar. That nothing like this occurred may be a measure of what the crisis has finally proved about global capital's recognition—as well as that of the other capitalist states—of the central role of the U.S. state in keeping the system going.

The Limits of Populism

The greatest political danger that both the banks and the state faced was the scandal over bonuses paid to managers in bailed-out firms, even as unemployment continued to climb and as banks refused loans to those they now deemed not credit-worthy. The real "moral hazard" this entailed was the fear this might lead to calls for permanent bank nationalization becoming widespread. But just as the Labour Government in the UK set up its provision of massive public capital to the banks in the fall of 2008 so that they would still "operate on a commercial basis at arm's length" from any government direction or control,[62] so did the U.S. Treasury, no less under Geithner than under Paulson, draw back from taking direct control over companies in which it became the major stockholder.

The Congressional furor which enveloped Geithner over the millions in bonuses paid to AIG executives within months of his taking office was directly related to the untenable position this put members of Congress who had insisted the crucial condition for putting public money into the car companies was that autoworkers' contracts be torn up and renegotiated. The obvious class bias this entailed went all the way back to the beginning of the neoliberal era when Volcker was put on the Chrysler board at the insistence of Congress to oversee UAW concessions during the Chrysler bail-out. The difference now was that the grotesque salaries and bonuses bankers paid themselves—which somehow had seemed acceptable when Wall Street was facilitating a new wave of capitalist globalization—could no longer be as easily defended by politicians after the very process of financialization had erupted to produce the crisis.

The incoming Obama administration appeared much more committed to rather more equitable distributional outcomes than its predecessor. Yet as one of the great Marxist theorists of the state, Ralph Miliband, put it in his 1969 book *The State in Capitalist Society*, "reform always and necessarily falls short of the promise it was proclaimed to hold: the crusades which were to reach 'new frontiers,' to create 'the great society,' to eliminate poverty, to assure justice for all."[63] What always lay behind this were the fears, reinforced by capitalist pressures, of aggravating a crisis of capital accumulation. It almost feels as though Miliband was speaking directly to those who were so enthusiastic about Obama when one reads:

> Such fears are well justified. But there is more than one way to deal with the adverse conditions which these new governments encounter on their assumption of office. One of them is to treat these conditions as a challenge to greater boldness, as an opportunity to greater radicalism, and as a means, rather than an obstacle, to swift and decisive measures of reform. There is, after all, much that a genuinely radical government, firm in purpose and enjoying a substantial measure of popular support, may hope to do on the morrow of its electoral legitimation, not despite crisis conditions but because of them. And doing so, it is also likely to receive the support of many people, hitherto uncommitted or half-committed, but willing to accept a resolute lead.[64]

The fact that the transformation of the state was most certainly nowhere on the Obama administration's agenda may have had less to do with Obama's reluctance to alienate the coalition of corporate and financial elites that helped finance his election campaign, than with their common embrace of the systemic structural linkages between capital and the state. The roots of this are much older and go much deeper than neoliberalism, although they became ever more blatant during that era.

Joining in the vilification of financiers has always been a central trope of the populism commonly practiced by American politicians. A particularly memorable instance of how U.S. elites have to accommodate to—and at the same time overcome—a populist political culture was Henry Paulson's declaration before the House Financial Services Committee, as he tried to get his TARP plan through Congress, that "the American people are angry about executive compensation and rightfully so."[65] This was rather rich given that he had been Wall Street's highest paid CEO, receiving $38.3 million in salary, stock and options in the year before joining the Treasury, plus a mid-year $18.7 million bonus on his departure as well as an estimated $200 million tax break against the sale of his almost $500 million share holding in Goldman Sachs—as was required to avoid conflict of interest in his new job.[66] When Paulson appeared before the Congressional hearings to defend his TARP plan to save the financial system, he acknowledged that Wall Street's exorbitant compensation schemes are a serious problem. But Paulson immediately added "we must find a way to address this in legislation *without undermining the effectiveness of the program*."[67]

The accommodation to the culture of populism was also seen at work in both McCain's and Obama's campaign rhetoric against greed and speculation (even though Wall Street investment banks were among their largest campaign contributors and supplied some of their key advisers). President Obama made the identical appeal as Paulson had six months earlier when his Treasury Secretary's new plan for leveraging private investments with massive public subsidies to save the financial system was rolled out amidst the mass outrage over the millions paid out to the very executives who had created the mess. "You've got a pretty egregious situation here that people are understandably upset about," Obama said, referring to these bonuses. "So let's see if there are ways of doing this that are both legal, that are constitutional, that uphold our basic principles of fairness, *but don't hamper us from getting the banking system back on track*."[68]

Like Paulson before him, Obama was signaling that really attacking the class inequality that is embedded in Wall Street would endanger working people's immediate interests in not losing what little they have as subordinate class participants in the financial system. Given that market efficiency could no longer credibly be claimed to explain why the basic principles of fairness should not be taken too far, Obama's "but" spoke volumes about how social justice is trumped by class hegemony in a capitalist society.

How ironic, but how typically so, that Obama should have made a show of calling the chief executives of twelve major financial institutions to the White House just before the end of 2009. The day before he had gone on television to proclaim "I did not run for office to be helping out a bunch of fat cat bankers." His main message to the bankers was that "America's banks received enormous assistance from American taxpayers to rebuild their industry—and now that they're back on their feet we expect an extraordinary commitment from them to help rebuild our economy... and create new jobs." As for financial sector reform Obama expressed his frustration over the "big gap between what I am hearing here in the White House and in the activities of lobbyists on behalf of those institutions."[69] As Goldman Sachs showed a surge in its net income for 2009 to a record $13.4 billion while unemployment remained stuck at over 10 per cent, Obama's frustration at the palpable political costs involved (which Goldman's promise to reduce its annual bonus pool from $22 billion to $16 billion and to donate $500 million to charities could do little to mollify) led him to announce two new measures in January 2010. One was a "Financial Crisis Responsibility Fee" on the largest banks projected to raise $90 billion over 10 years. The other, prominently associated with Paul Volcker's reform proposals in 2009,[70] was to prohibit deposit taking banks from proprietary activities (i.e. using their own capital to speculate as well as operate their own hedge funds).

The Fed and Treasury's lack of enthusiasm for even such modest reforms had less to do with the activities of lobbyists than the problematic implications for a highly integrated financial system. The responsibility fee had implications for the "repo market" in U.S. Treasury securities, which would limit lending by banks and complicate the practice of monetary policy. And isolating banks' own proprietary trading would be very difficult given how much of their capital was necessarily involved in helping clients carry out trades in stocks, bonds, and derivatives. The integration of commercial and investment banking combined with the integration of the American state and financial markets in global capitalism makes any return to the watertight compartments of the "Glass-Steagall" New Deal reforms impossible. Even Volcker spoke not in terms of reviving Glass-Steagall but only returning to its "spirit" and this was reflected in the vagueness of Obama's proposals.

As with the 1930s reforms—which the banks were closely involved in devising and implementing, and which became the foundation for the recovery and enormous expansion of U.S. banking—the final form taken by these much more limited measures, which touch on a small fraction of the revenues of the big banks, are as likely to strengthen Wall Street as weaken it. The financial crisis of the first decade of the 21st century afforded an opportunity which could have been used by a genuinely radical government to nationalize the banks and turn them into a democratic public utility. This opportunity was wasted. Its displacement in 2010 with minor reforms presented in a way that led to headlines like "Obama Declares War on Wall Street" and "Banks Face Revolutionary Reform," captures the essence of populism, and bespeaks its limits.[71]

CHAPTER FIVE

FROM FINANCE TO INDUSTRY: THE CRISIS IN AUTO

The profits from U.S. industry were relatively high in the years leading up to the crisis of 2007–08 and balance sheets were generally strong, which limited the depth of the economic collapse brought on by the crisis. But there were important exceptions to this generalization, the most significant of which was the auto industry. For some time before the crisis, General Motors, Ford, and Chrysler—once the "Big Three" but now less respectfully tagged as the "Detroit Three"—had watched their market share and profits plummet. Overall economic uncertainty, coupled with the sensitivity of auto sales to the freezing up of credit and to the type of speculation that pushed up oil prices in the winter of 2007–8, drove consumers from showrooms. The very survival of the U.S.-based auto companies was suddenly in jeopardy.

Of all 20th century industries, the auto sector had best captured the sway of capitalism and the rise of American dominance over the world market. The assembly line showed off capitalism's remarkable productive potential and the automobile flaunted capitalism's consumerist possibilities. At mid-century, with Europe and Japan emerging from the devastation of war, 80 percent of the world's cars traveled on North America roads. In this context, catching up to the U.S. example became a common aspiration across the developed capitalist countries.

For those who built the cars and trucks, the fruits of the assembly line were not, of course, automatically passed on. That only came as workers organized to challenge the unilateral power of their employers. The United Auto Workers (UAW) achieved its breakthrough and inspired others through the creative sit-down strikes and by introducing to this iconic industry the principle of industrial unionism—a form of unionism representing the unskilled as well as the skilled and uniting workers across companies. In the growth years after the war, the proudest achievement of the UAW and then the Canadian Auto Workers (CAW)—even to the point of trading off workplace rights—was winning what was essentially a private welfare state. Over and above their wage increases, workers achieved the security of a range of benefits, of which healthcare and pensions were the most significant.

In the seventy-seven years before the fateful events of 2008, General Motors (GM) was the largest of the large in the auto industry. During that long reign, the aphorism attributed to GM President Charlie Wilson—"What's good for General Motors is good for the country"—seemed, in spite of its arrogance, apt.[72] As early as the 1920s, GM had pioneered the multidivisional corporation—a form of corporate organization that allowed for both the centralization (of planning) and the decentralization (of execution) that was so crucial to facilitating the post-war omnipresence of global corporations. As late as 2000, *Fortune* ranked GM as the largest corporation in the world as measured by revenue.[73]

From very early on, GM was not only a producer of vehicles but also a major financial company. In 1919, GM introduced its own financial arm, the General Motors Acceptance Corporation (GMAC), to support its dealers and sales. By 1985 GMAC had financed 100 million vehicles and was branching into real estate and mortgages. A new division within GMAC, Residential Capital (ResCap), soon extended to ten global locations and "purchased loans in the secondary market from a variety of originators (for example, mortgage bankers) and sold them as mortgage-backed securities (MBS) to fixed-income institutional investors."[74]

Finance also directly affected GM's productive operations. The easy availability of credit in the 1980s and 1990s led GM to flirt with a number of (ultimately ill-fated) diversifications and to develop a strategy to revive profits through the sale of expensive but highly profitable trucks to consumers enticed by low-interest loans—a strategy which, in assuming that oil prices would stay low and the economy strong, blurred the line between productive and financial "speculation." Financial markets affected production as well through the pressures for higher returns, which translated into demands for worker concessions, tighter work standards, and the outsourcing of components (downsizing). And it was financial markets that provided the funds for suppliers of the components—like Delphi—to ambitiously expand and sometimes over-expand.[75]

Beyond credit, GM now directly participated in financial markets as a primary agent. It regularly lent and borrowed overnight anywhere in the world to maximize the company's use of cash via arbitrage operations. As a global corporation facing a wide range of uncertainties, GM bought and sold financial derivatives to minimize risks from fluctuations in exchange rates and commodity prices and, to a lesser degree, in inflation and interest rates.

It might be asked whether all of this—the relative strength of GM's financial arm and GM's role in financial markets, alongside the collapse of GM's profits and its downsizing as a vehicle producer—implied that GM has been converted into an essentially financial company, but the answer would have to be a negative one. As important as GM's financial involvement has been, its principle pursuit has remained accumulation through hiring and coordinating workers to produce vehicles. The financial dimension is important, but its prime role has been that of supplementing and facilitating GM as a producer of vehicles.

GM could not have extended its international operations as aggressively and successfully without the contributions of finance to insuring against various kinds of risk (exchange rates being the most prominent). And though the Volcker shock with its higher interest rates—devastating auto sales and increasing the cost of corporate credit when it was most needed—might have been expected to create intense tensions between the auto industry and finance, they shared a consensus on this move to neoliberalism. That concurrence was evident again in the absence of substantive conflicts between industry and finance during the latest crisis. The glue is a shared social relationship to labor. While finance certainly disciplines industry, this is part of the fundamental disciplining of labor to the end of ultimately increasing profits for both industrial and financial capitalists.[76] Finance has not only provided credit to workers, which served to support markets for goods and services, but also opened the door much wider to workers viewing their homes and pensions as "investments," further contributing to labor's tighter integration into capitalist social relations.

And then, on June 1, 2008—exactly 100 years after Henry Ford had introduced the auto assembly line—the previously unimaginable happened: the lines at General Motors fell silent. When GM came out of bankruptcy some six weeks later it, like Chrysler, had been saved by the intervention of the American state. The federal loans passed on to GM totaled over $50 billion, some of which was converted to equity giving the U.S. government a 60 percent stake in the company; this was supplemented by almost $10 billion from Canadian governments, most of which was converted to a 12 percent stake. The UAW health trust (VEBA) was given a 17.5 percent stake for the contributions made by autoworker concessions, leaving private investors with slightly more than a 10 percent stake.

The American state's majority ownership did not, however, come with any intention to convert GM to some larger social purpose. Though insisting that as part of getting its survival funds GM close plants, restructure its operations and management, lay off workers and enforce major concessions on the workforce, the American state took a "hands-off" approach to how the "New GM" would conducts it business and returns to profit.[77] The government would, it declared, sell its shares and exit formal ownership as soon as possible.

The humbling of General Motors as an icon of American culture and power raises various questions and an especially common one has been whether this represented a failure specific to GM and the U.S. auto industry, or speaks to the decline of U.S. manufacturing more generally and with it, American economic power. But, as we'll argue, a more important issue—because it is so central to the *challenging* of U.S. power both at home and abroad—is the extent to which the losses imposed on the auto unions reflected a momentous defeat of the broader working class in both the U.S. and Canada.

Competition and Globalization

The crisis of General Motors must be placed in the context of global competition. The auto industry has become global in scope but remains primarily regional in the organization of production. The major companies have come to compete across the globe, but while they traded across regions, direct investment in facilities abroad was the principal means for penetrating those specific regions (North America, Europe, Asia, and Latin America).

Such cross-investment has had three implications. First, it generated a base of public support within each region for "free trade." For example, communities in the U.S. South—which saw themselves as benefiting from Japanese and European investment and the trade in certain components this implies—shied away from "protectionism." Capitalism consequently tends to create both increased competition between states *and* their mutual integration. Second, entry by investment in large plants, as opposed to shipping vehicles from under-utilized plants, tended to reinforce the constant formation of sectoral excess capacity. Plants closed but new ones reappeared in the hope of outcompeting others. Third, the consequent competition was very intense and one particular dimension of that competition was "outsourcing"—moving work that was formerly done in-house to lower-cost specialized firms in other parts of the broad region (in the case of the U.S. and Canada, to rural areas, the American South, Mexico, and to some extent abroad).

Capitalist competition implies winners and losers and a constant restructuring of not just work, jobs and communities, but of class relations. While competition destroys individual businesses, and may include a period of crises in particular sectors, at the end of the day capitalists as a class have emerged more powerful out of this process. The survival of the fittest meant that some companies come out of the competition more robust than ever, better positioned to restore profits and investment, and able to take over the market shares of those driven out.

For the working classes, however, greater competition meant something quite different. Global "competitiveness" has been the greatest disciplinary force confronting workers (directly in the private sector, indirectly in the public sector): "compete or you lose your job and livelihood; compete or our country won't be able to afford its social programs." As the competition between companies was translated into competition among workers, workers were pushed to identify with their own employer, while undermining each other in the desperation to hang on to their jobs. Competition consequently fragmented the working class. It eroded their one ultimate strength—solidarity.

The increasing internationalization of capitalism intensified that competition. But how was it that the Japanese companies, once so far behind, came to be the ones moving to the front while the U.S. companies fell into crisis? It is not enough to assert that the Japanese were simply smarter: we need to appreciate the context in which this historic reversal occurred. An immediate question is how the Japanese companies were allowed into the U.S. and Canada, while Japan itself remained virtually closed to outside companies. Answering this requires us to bring some history of the development of globalization, and particularly the American empire, into the story.

Though often viewed as inevitable, globalization in fact had to be *made*. Not only General Motors but also the American state was at the center of this making. It is true that capitalists, driven by the goal of expanding profits and the pressures of competition, are disposed—as Marx noted—to "go anywhere, settle anywhere." But capitalist states, concerned to defend their own capital, have often tended to act as a barrier to globalization. While individual capitalists reached outward, in the pre-World War One era this occurred alongside drives to divide the world into national empires and, especially among emerging capitalist powers, attempts to protect their markets through tariffs. In the first half of the 20th century, marked by the two world wars and the collapse of trade and free capital flows during the Great Depression, this divisive nationalism went so far that a globalized capitalism seemed impossible.

During the course of World War II, the American state—conscious of these past failures, aware of its unique standing after the war, and acting in the interests of its own capital—set out to remake the world in a way that facilitated the making of a global capitalism. It was especially concerned to reconstitute capitalism in Europe and Japan, but to do so in a way that kept them open to American capital. As the U.S. integrated foreign capitalists into this project, it created new competitors.

Consistency in pushing for the priority of the "open-door" abroad implied that the U.S. would move to an open door policy for imports and investment at home. In the particular case of Japan, the fact of the Cold War and the centrality of Japan to the penetration of capitalism into Asia, led the U.S. to accept a certain "flexibility" in mutual international economic relations. Japan was permitted to restrict foreign investment, yet access foreign technology; to maintain, into the mid-

1980s, an undervalued currency; and it was allowed to restrict entry into its market, yet retain full access to the U.S. market. (At the time, in the post-war years, it should be noted, Japan was only a semi-industrialized country with a limited market for consumer goods.)

While still under U.S. occupation, the Japanese state and corporations had smashed the militant Japanese trade unions by the early 1950s, with the auto sector being a crucial battleground. By the 1970s, Japan—with borrowed or bought technology and the competitive advantages of lower wages—was making significant inroads into the U.S. auto market. Japan's exports of small, fuel efficient and relatively inexpensive cars meshed with what U.S. consumers were looking for in a period of elevated energy prices and economic stagnation and inflation. When Japanese imports increased especially fast and the U.S. government moved to limit them, the Japanese corporations got the message and moved to directly produce inside the United States.

The Japanese auto companies quickly proved that they could compete as effectively without the cost and so-called cultural advantages of Japan. They could match or surpass the competitiveness of General Motors, Ford, and Chrysler even while producing *within* North America. By the end of the century, they had captured half the U.S. and Canadian car markets and were serious challengers in truck production. Well before the "Great Financial Crisis" that unfolded in 2008 and forced GM and Chrysler into bankruptcy, the Detroit Three were in serious trouble.[78]

General Motors and Toyota

The explanations of why GM, in particular, failed range from its complacency in light of past successes to the failures of its models in terms of styling, quality and price. Other explanations faulted its size, which came with a degree of bureaucratization that hindered cooperation across departments and left GM's responses to market changes too rigid; or blamed GM for giving in too easily to union demands and thus suffering from lower productivity and higher costs. Most recently, criticism has focused on GM's short-term concentration on SUVs and trucks and its corresponding insensitivity to the environment as a critical market factor. There is of course something to most, if not all, these criticisms. Yet GM's failures relative to Toyota should be placed in a wider context—not least to avoid romanticizing Toyota and pointing to "Toyotaism" as the solution.

That it was the Japanese corporations that eventually brought such vehicles to North America was less a matter of foresight than of necessity. The Japanese market, based on relatively low incomes and high gas prices, supported the development of a capacity to build small cars, while in the 1970s and 1980s the Japanese auto companies couldn't compete technologically with the Detroit Three in larger, more sophisticated vehicles. As the Japanese companies moved upscale they were soon as anxious as the U.S.-based companies to move into higher-profit larger vehicles (in China, GM actually led Toyota in emphasizing small car production).[79] Moreover, what passes for greater productivity at the Japanese transplants includes a greater repression of their non-union workforce: management flexibility at the expense of any worker flexibility, inhumane line-speeds, discarding injured workers who can no longer sustain the work-pace. (Additionally, as we'll elaborate below, the Japanese transplants in North America benefited competitively from the uneven effects of the U.S. being the only developed country without socialized healthcare costs.)

As for GM, its emphasis on SUVs and trucks in the 1990s was precisely what it was being pressured to do by shareholders hungry for higher returns, including institutional investors like pension funds. With their traditional bias for larger vehicles fortified by relatively low gas prices, U.S. consumers were ready to pay big bucks for big vehicles, and all companies were only too happy to comply with "the market." This could, of course, not last forever and when the market changed (especially the doubling of oil prices between early 2007 and the summer of 2008 coinciding with the eruption of the financial crisis) GM and the other U.S.-based companies couldn't make the transition rapidly enough to smaller, more fuel-efficient vehicles.[80]

In terms of autoworkers' wages, GM's problems were not rooted in exorbitant gains. The UAW made their great strides in the 1950s and 1960s. Since the end of the 1970s they, like other workers, have generally been on the defensive. Productivity in U.S. motor vehicle assembly, for example, has almost doubled since 1990, yet real wages have remained virtually constant, and in the parts sector they have actually fallen by about 6 percent. In any case, while imports from Japan originally had the advantage of lower wage costs, the Japanese assembly plants that came to the U.S. more or less matched the wages of the Detroit Three to avoid unionization. But benefits, and particularly health care costs, were a different story.

The driving factor in the escalation of costs was not primarily the gains negotiated in collective agreements. Rather, it was the extraordinary increases in costs for the *same* benefits. Inflationary pressures, in other words, didn't come from autoworkers but from the drug companies and private health insurers providing and profiting from these benefits.[81] Rising healthcare costs affect vehicle prices and sales. But if all companies faced the same costs, no company would be relatively disadvantaged. It is because the U.S. healthcare system is overwhelmingly private that the impact is so uneven. Even if the transplants were unionized and had the same benefits, their shorter period in the U.S. (and consequent lower number of retirees receiving healthcare benefits) meant that the transplants would still have a competitive advantage over U.S.-based companies.[82]

The gap is stunning. At the end of the 1970s, GM had some 470,000 hourly workers and 133,000 retirees and surviving spouses. In 2009, at the time of its bankruptcy, the workforce had decreased by over 85 percent (to 64,000) while the number of retirees had increased almost four-fold (to some *half a million*) as GM became one of the largest healthcare consumer in the U.S. From a ratio of fewer than 3 retirees per 10 active workers, GM had gone to 77 retirees per 10 active workers. This was hardly sustainable, especially when the Japanese transplants collectively—Toyota, Honda, Nissan, and Subaru—had less than 1000 retirees in the United States.

Pensions were a slightly different matter. Unlike healthcare costs, they were paid out of a stand-alone fund. Company payments were invested in stocks and bonds, and as long as the payments continued and the returns generated were high, there was no problem. But what seemed adequate during the stock market boom of the 1990s, changed quickly and dramatically when—at the same time that GM was increasingly less able to set aside new monies—the returns on the assets in the pension funds collapsed. Relative to GM's falling workforce and shrinking market, the burden of both healthcare and pensions was all the greater.

For workers, this dependence on their employers for healthcare and pensions—as opposed to receiving them from the state as a right—pushed them toward lobbying governments to support these corporations and, alongside this, vulnerable to government or corporate calls for concessions. Moreover, in trying to gain public support for their dilemma, autoworkers found themselves relatively isolated since most workers didn't get such benefits. Perhaps most significantly, while it once could be assumed that the largest corporations would be around forever and so pension promises were safe, that era—eclipsed by the intensification of competition over the past quarter century—is gone. Even the biggest private companies can no longer guarantee workers their benefits.

Misdiagnosis: Reciprocity, Hollowing Out, and U.S. Declinism

When we consider what kind of intervention might have been proposed to deal with the impact on autoworkers and their communities, certain perspectives on the crisis lead to confused if not harmful strategies. The Canadian Auto Workers, for example, has for some time put emphasis on calling for "trade reciprocity": where foreign-based corporations are accessing North American markets, their home markets should in turn be opened to North American exports. This sounds fair enough, but it misunderstands the nature of globalization. If Asian markets were in fact opened, this would do nothing for Canadian jobs. The auto companies would still be uncompetitive with Asian wages and unwilling to ship from the U.S. and Canada. On the other hand, if it were made easier for companies like GM to invest in Asia and organize their parts flows across that region, this would be beneficial to GM—but would hardly be a solution for workers in North America.

What is of special concern (since the policy itself won't help) is the ideological content of focusing on trade reciprocity as a union strategy. The CAW was a leader in the earlier fight against free trade and still officially opposes it on the grounds that enforcing the property rights of corporations—the freedom to produce, move and sell where they please—undermines the freedom of workers to shape their lives and societies. The demand for reciprocity, however, contradicts this position: calling for other countries to become more economically open further *legitimates* free trade.

A related misconception lies in seeing the crisis in terms of the "hollowing out" of U.S. industrial capacities as entire sectors moved abroad. It is easy to understand why, based on their direct experience, workers might see things this way. But the fact is that jobs are not only going, but also coming in (though generally not coming to the same places that were left). This is especially so in the auto industry. The Detroit Three were investing in rural areas and the U.S. South even as they closed plants elsewhere.[83] And the facilities that have undermined the Detroit Three have increasingly been new foreign-based investments—assembly and parts plants that are now here, in the U.S. and Canada, rather than abroad.

All this is better understood as a sweeping *restructuring* of the industry, rather than its hollowing out. Workplaces were made leaner and more productive and components were outsourced as part of a geographic relocation of the industry within, and not just away from, North America. Large investments by foreign-based companies inside North America, and not just imports, were the main contributors to the radical shifts in market shares. This came with a lowering of unionization, a weakening of the unions that remained, a lowering of worker expectations and consequently a restructuring of class relations. (The restructuring in auto was itself part of a more general transfer of jobs from manufacturing to services and within manufacturing, to higher tech.)

One aspect of these domestic transformations is that it wasn't imports that were causing the majority of job losses in the U.S. and Canada. Rather—over and above the loss of market share to the transplants producing domestically—it was the outsourcing of components to domestic suppliers and productivity gains due to speedup and the introduction of labor-saving technological change. For example, in 1990–2005, U.S. output in the auto industry as a whole, including the transplants, increased by an average of 3.1 percent annually in vehicle assembly and 4.8 percent in parts (the latter benefited form the outsourcing). But productivity in assembly (3.7 percent) grew faster than output and almost as fast in parts (4.4 percent). Thus overall employment fell. For GM alone, sales fell by some 10 percent over this period but employment fell by ⅔. The significance of the impact of productivity is especially clear in the computer equipment sector, where output increased by a remarkable 22 percent per year, yet with productivity growing even faster (28 percent annually), employment fell by an average of 5 percent annually.[84]

A third misconception is that the bankruptcies of GM and Chrysler, along with the financial crisis, signal the end of U.S. global leadership and its replacement by China, Asia, or Europe. The implication is that the U.S. is doomed to a period of economic decline and/or with an expectation that this decline will lead to some dramatic and progressive response. Consider first the financial crisis. It certainly demonstrates how chaotic and anti-social capitalism is as an economic system. But if anything, it *confirms* U.S. imperial leadership. The crisis was based in the U.S. yet, posturing aside, no country and no investors saw fit to get out of dollars. The dollar generally was, in these times of trouble, the universal safe haven and the centrality of U.S. leadership within an interdependent capitalism remains clear.

As for the auto sector, it is no longer the measure it once was of U.S. economic strength. That has shifted to other higher tech sectors and the pervasiveness of U.S. business services, including—despite the financial crisis—financial services (for instance, Goldman Sachs, JP Morgan, and Citigroup still far outranked all other banks around the world in mergers and acquisitions services right through 2008, and indeed were joined by Morgan Stanley and Bank of America in the world's top five in 2009). Moreover, U.S. auto companies do remain an international force. Though slipping to second world-wide, GM—freed of its debt, having transferred the risks of healthcare to workers, having won massive concessions from the workers, and concentrating on its most productive plants and successful models—remains for now the largest auto producer in the U.S. and a leader in the auto industries of Russia, China, and Latin America. At the same time, the investments of the Japanese companies in the U.S. do not reflect American decline but highlight the continuing importance of operating in the heart of the empire because of the size of its market and the political limits of market penetration through imports. Toyota sells more vehicles in the U.S. than in Japan, over half of Honda's global profits come from the U.S. market, and these foreign-based companies have, if reluctantly at first, come to invest not only in assembly plants but also in parts plants and a measure of research and development.

A crucial part of the strength of U.S. capital and the U.S. state lie in the weaknesses of its labor movement, which provides, as this crisis has sadly shown, the U.S. elite with the flexibility it needs to solve its problems on terms favorable to it. Had U.S. workers demonstrated a capacity to limit concessions or foreclosures, to demand a democratization of the banks rather than simply "fixing" them, to insist on a radical correction in the gross inequalities that emerged on the way to this crisis, to focus on rebuilding social infrastructures and cities rather than simply "stimulus," the crisis would have confronted much deeper uncertainties—and a more ambitious and far-reaching set of alternatives might have reached the public agenda.

Toward a Class Perspective

The crisis seriously weakened GM, put Chrysler into the hands of Fiat, and destroyed hundreds of auto parts companies. Yet at the end of the day there will still be an auto industry in North America that is more concentrated (with fewer but larger corporations) and, in capitalist terms, stronger than it has been in recent years. But the workers in the industry have been dramatically weakened and in light of the high profile of the sector and the historic role of its key unions (as well of course of the depth of the current crisis itself), the outcome in auto will clearly escalate pressures on other workers, both private and public. To that extent, the defeat of the autoworkers threatens to become a historic *class* defeat.

Both the UAW and CAW have, unlike in their early days, refused to raise any larger questions about the economic system. In fact, in the name of job security the unions (and their members) generally *defended* the corporations against any criticism, such as that of corporate insensitivity to environmental sustainability. This lack of independence from the corporations has cost workers not just in terms of the unions' public credibility and leadership role on social issues but it has, in its short sightedness, ultimately left autoworkers *less* secure. Moreover, as the crisis unfolded and the jobs issue dominated all other considerations even more, the union—absent any alternatives for defending jobs—was left all the more vulnerable to the most damaging concessions. And even when corporations like GM and Chrysler were saved, most jobs were not, since a basic part of the corporate (and government) recovery strategy included the further decimation of the workforce.

A fundamental lesson of the auto crisis, crucial to all workers, revolves around the cost of not having an independent class vision. Independent, that is, from employers and the competitive logic of capitalism, and confident in the collective potential of workers—union and non-union, employed and unemployed—to build a society supportive of equality, solidarity, and the deepest democratization of every dimension of society, especially of the economy itself. Limiting the analysis to specific issues and ignoring the wider context—that is, the development of global capitalism as a social system—leads to incomplete solutions and incomplete solutions can in fact make things worse. It is the refusal to think in larger terms, typically in the name of being "realistic," which bears a good deal of the responsibility for why workers were left so vulnerable when the auto crisis hit and why they subsequently found themselves boxed into such narrow options.

Escaping that debilitating trap—which involves *truly* being realistic—would mean learning to think and act in fresher, bigger, and more radical ways. This does not, of course, reduce basic workplace, bargaining, and union issues to a secondary status. Rather, it emphasizes that these can advance working class struggles only if located within a larger strategy for social change. In previous periods of economic turmoil, workers developed new structures for fighting back and visions of moving beyond the narrow confines of capitalism. It is to a broader discussion of the impasse in labor—the barriers and challenges to the revival and development of organized labor as a social force—that we now turn.

CHAPTER SIX

LABOR'S IMPASSE AND THE LEFT

If we are to do more than hope for the crisis to be over so we can return to a capitalism that didn't address our needs earlier, and more than passively watch as capitalism narrows our lives even further, then a new historical project must be placed on the agenda. And if this is to happen, organized labor will have to be one of the central agents in advancing it. Historically, trade unions have been one of the most effective social movements for the advancement of social justice in capitalist societies. Unionization was one of the first means through which workers struggled to improve wages and increase their control in workplaces as they bargained with the owners of capital. Unions have also been a key vehicle by which workers have campaigned, typically in conjunction with socialist parties, for the extension of democracy through the advocacy of the vote for all adults, civil rights such as freedoms of association, assembly and dissent, and the universalization of social programs to meet the basic social needs of all. All these struggles for social justice were opposed by the capitalist classes. It is only through a great deal of ideological obfuscation and re-writing of history that market freedoms can be equated with the development of political freedoms.

It is impossible to separate analytically or politically the defeat of working class politics and unions after the radicalizations of the

1960s and 1970s from the emergence of neoliberalism as a set of policy proposals of the New Right in the early 1980s. From the outset, neoliberal policies came with a political focus: to overturn the efforts being made by unions and Left parties to establish greater economic democracy in enterprises and democratic determination of economic and social priorities at the level of the state.[85]

Neoliberal policies in North America sought to attack and restrict the rights of workers and their capacity to form unions. The goal was to re-establish capitalist control over workplaces, restrain wages and transform state policy so as to insulate the state from popular pressures that might extend workers' and community rights over plant shutdowns and investment. At the same time, private property rights were extended into as many spheres as possible, including into the public sector through various measures to "marketize" public administration and public goods.

In practice, neoliberal labor policies have legislated and implemented a range of legal and regulatory obstacles to union organizing, use of the right to strike and on political activism.[86] North American unions also faced a squeeze on wages and public sector austerity to restore the profitability of capitalist firms. These policies were supplemented by labor market policies for "flexibility." Workers were to be compelled to become more dependent upon the market as individuals so as to limit their ability to contest the social relations of the capitalist market as a class. As we have argued in earlier chapters, this strategy also came to mean increasing working class dependence on financial markets.

The consolidation of neoliberalism across the 1990s saw the policy agenda expand in ambition and scope, particularly as social democratic parties (and the American Democratic Party) began to incorporate neoliberal policies into their programs. These parties—the so-called political arm of the labor movement—began to rule as neoliberals once in power. A good example of this policy realignment was, of course, the Presidency of Bill Clinton in the 1990s (who was supported throughout by the AFL-CIO). As a result, the capacity of unions to advance their traditional redistributive policy agenda for social justice collapsed.

Another factor shifting the balance of power toward the capitalist classes was the mass adoption of the new production technologies in both the manufacturing and service sectors. They were deployed in ways that intensified work, extended management control over labor processes, and increased global competition. Unions became decidedly weaker in making gains in collective bargaining. Organizing and defending new members, especially those in new service sector employment and migrant workers, was proving to be exceedingly difficult using traditional organizing techniques, particularly with the advantages neoliberal policies had bestowed on managers.

The political climate since September 2001 in North America, along with slower economic growth, military interventions by the NATO countries and hard right governments clamping-down on political dissent, has been even more hostile toward unions. The small steps by unions toward an alliance with a fledgling anti-globalization movement—just as it was beginning to form new organizing capacities around sweatshops and service sector work and an anti-capitalist ideology—led nowhere. Rather than rethinking the nature of neoliberal globalization and the lack of union strategic and organizational capacities to respond to it, the North American union movement retreated, turning inward to ever more narrowly focused trade union issues. As the financial crisis ripped across the economy, unions were barely beginning to face up to their predicament. In the U.S. case, the 2005 split from the AFL-CIO by the Change-to-Win Federation has accomplished next-to-nothing with both suffering a drop in total members—never mind the falling share of the total labor force in unions—in the subsequent period.[87]

The political and economic setting facing the union movement today is, perhaps, the most difficult since the Great Depression. The "disorganization" of the old working class institutions—the trade unions, labor parties, co-operatives, benefit societies, even "labor temples" that were once at the center of working class community life—is one of the most formidable obstacles to both thinking about and establishing an alternative to neoliberalism. It is necessary to make a deeper assessment of the impact of neoliberalism on the labor movement and the prospects for a new union politics before turning to a wider discussion of the renewal of the Left.

The Challenges before Unions

A first challenge that unions face has been the major restructuring of factories, as capital regained control over labor processes and its ability to deploy investment funds without restraint. Beginning with the economic slowdown of the 1970s, and particularly after the Volcker shock in the U.S. in 1981–82 radically drove up world interest rates to force an economic restructuring deep enough to break workers' wage expectations and power, an "employers' offensive" ensued across the advanced capitalist countries. Employers began a series of labor-saving plant shutdowns and a major shift of production to locales with lower union density, such as the southern U.S. and northern Mexico in the case of North America.

Further workplace restructuring continued through the 1990s. In the realm of work, the so-called "new economy" referred to a rise in service sector employment, especially to work in the information and communications technology (ICT) sector, and the mass growth of various kinds of low-paid service work. Labor processes were now characterized by lean production organizational norms, flexible manufacturing systems, non-standard work arrangements, and extensive resort to cheap migrant labor pools and temporary worker programs. The employers' offensive and much higher levels of unemployment and precarious jobs meant that competition between workers increased as well, particularly as migration and rising participation of women in the labor force changed the character of the working classes, and neither union or political organization was developing in a way that could solidify the development of new working class institutions across these social identities and diverse work spaces.

Workplace controls and the increased pressure on wages have posed a second challenge for unions: how to sustain their power to bargain collectively. The entire period of neoliberalism has, for instance, seen a remarkable degree of wage and income polarization and especially widening gaps between capital's share and labor's share of total income. The legislative and juridical restrictions on union organizing and free collective bargaining are key constraints on union's capacities. Union weakness has also provided employers with the opportunity to overhaul union agreements to give management increased flexibility in terms of over hiring and firing, and wages and benefits as well as control over the labor process. The specific ways this has been institutionalized across the capitalist countries is quite diverse. In Europe, for example, it has taken the form of competitive corporatism in which unions agree to increase company competitiveness through wage restraint, cooperating in new work arrangements and signing long-term contracts. Depending upon the specific relationship to the state, this has taken different national forms—the "shared austerity" of Sweden, the "co-managed austerity" of Germany, the "administered austerity" of France, and so on.

In traditional manufacturing strongholds in North America, unions like the United Steelworkers have also engaged in "partnership" and "co-management" schemes through long term contracts that give up the right to strike and lock in work arrangements which give management more flexibility and control as a trade-off for some job protection and union security. And to finally gain union recognition from longstanding non-unionized companies, some unions—like the SEIU and CAW, for example—have even given up the right to strike altogether. This was a variation of "voluntary recognition agreements" that have been occurring in the service sector across North America, most often after long unsuccessful organizing campaigns. The corporation agrees to recognize the union rather than to continue to suffer extensive damage to the corporate image and loss of management time. The union, in turn, gains a contract but also agrees to certain workplace and bargaining concessions that restricts future bargaining and organizational possibilities.

A third challenge for unions has been how governments have themselves adopted "flexibility" as their main policy objective in dealing with labor markets. Neoliberal policy explicitly rejects Keynesian policies geared towards full employment of the workforce in favor of prioritizing policies that keep inflation down. This takes the form of restrictive monetary policies aimed at ensuring that aggregate wage increases are kept more or less in line with low rate of inflation. This policy essentially also ensures that the majority of productivity gains being made in the economy are claimed by employers as profits, not workers. Market discipline is further bolstered by maintaining a "natural rate of unemployment": a pool of workers free to take up new jobs, particularly low-wage work in the service sector, as it becomes available. Another component of flexible policies has been restricting access to, and reducing benefits for, programs such as unemployment insurance or social assistance on the grounds that they discourage people from accepting low paid jobs, and accepting lower work standards to keep their jobs.

The economic crisis is intensifying a number of the detrimental longer-term trends encouraged by this policy regime: decreasing real wages, increasing precarious and marginal work, undermining public sector services and employment, and increasing reliance on migrant workers with restricted rights. Employers are emboldened to step up their campaigns against unionization and further pursue their efforts to increase insecurity and exploitation in the workplace under the label of "flexibility." This is what lies behind the major employer efforts to rollback pensions at the state level and redefine or even scrap pension benefits at the company level. The cuts occurring to health-care benefit provisions are another example. It would not be a stretch to characterize the collective bargaining and policy regime that has faced American unions as one of "punitive austerity."

The internationalization of capital and the global reorganization of labor processes has been a fourth challenge for unions. One of the most important innovations has been the expansion of "international production networks," linking labor processes across several countries, with each providing a component of a finished product. This gives multinational corporations greater capacity to determine the allocation of capital and jobs internationally. In particular, corporations have gained a capacity to locate repetitive and ecologically damaging labor processes in poorer countries where low wages can be paid and the costs of ecological damage ignored. But the corporations can also shift high "value-added" activities, i.e. those that involve high skills at higher pay, to places where union strength is much weaker in order to allow the introduction of new labor processes with less interference from workers. In all of these cases, the internationalization of capital and the spatial reorganization of labor processes increase the leverage of employers over workers through the threat of capital moving elsewhere. Not only is labor relatively less mobile than capital, despite increasing migration, but union organization and capacity built up at particular worksites is not easily transferred.

The World Trade Organization (WTO) and international trade agreements such as NAFTA, as well as the political arrangements of the European Union, all are primarily designed to secure free capital mobility and protect property rights for multinational corporations and banks. Moreover, they often contain clauses that constrain states from adopting industrial policies, including those that might allow states at any level to assert greater control over investment. These agreements provide a political and legal architecture that in particular facilitates the internationalization of capital in the form of production networks. This was explicitly part of the logic of the establishment of NAFTA and the expansion of low-wage labor processes in Mexico. Workers in Mexico, for example, earn about one-tenth or less of the wages of workers in Canada and the U.S. for similar work. The initial period of NAFTA saw some two million less-skilled jobs relocated to Mexico, particularly to the *maquila* free trade zones in the northern border states. Parallel global pressures have hit Mexican workers, and indeed all workers, by the massive shift of so much of the world's manufacturing capacity to China and other low-wage Asian countries over the last decade. The internationalization of capital, facilitated by the trade liberalization and new trade rules that capital has called for, in turn compels all employers to drive down their labor costs.

Indeed, unless unions develop new strategies and organizational strength, competition between firms will continue to fuel competition between workers. This further shifts the balance of power in favor of employers. As seen in the case of UAW bargaining with the Detroit Three during the auto crisis, it is the competitiveness of the corporation—defined in their terms—that comes to dominate union policy. The inequalities and divisions between workers become not only sharper, but they are embedded in the very logic of union organization and strategy. With this form of "competitive unionism" becoming prevalent, union democracy, mobilization capacity, and ideological independence from employers all atrophy.

New Struggles, New Movement?

The class warfare from above inherent in neoliberalism put union movements across the advanced capitalist countries on the defensive. More than a dozen core capitalist economies have seen an absolute decline in union membership. In the case of both Canadian and U.S. unions, it is hard not to conclude that it has meant a decisive defeat. Union density in the U.S. has precipitously declined to just over one in ten workers being in a union today, while in Canada it is only three in ten. These figures reflect, in part, the difficulty of organizing the service sector, where about 80 percent of employment is now found. They also speak to a much wider decline of working class politics that has not encouraged the renewal of the labor movement.

Despite all these major difficulties, key struggles and signs of political resistance keep surfacing from both inside the labor movement and also broader social movements, revealing a vast potential for exploring new tactics for working class community as well as union mobilization.[88] In North America, some of this has come from "living wage" struggles led by local labor councils in major cities, in alliance with community groups, to reach out to the low-waged and unorganized, who are predominantly women and people of color. The mass immigrant rights May Day protests, as well as the day-to-day campaigns for the protection of undocumented workers, have taken place outside the main union movements, but they have also led to new linkages and alliances between many community groups and unions. Similar types of struggles are helping to rebuild local labor movements in many countries. After being beaten down by neoliberal attacks, the central labor federations have recognized—at times, even with a sense of urgency—the need to focus on organizing in new communities and sectors. Resolutions at union conventions on organizing, mobilizing and political issues have reflected this. A defensive and weak leadership means, however, that there is still an enormous distance to go in translating convention sentiment into organized political action. But the successes of these grassroots campaigns directed at low-waged workers suggest a significant opening for rebuilding the labor movement.

The "Great Recession" has led to a major drop-off in employment. Workplace layoffs and closures in the manufacturing sector have further undermined "good jobs" in core union strongholds. The layoffs spread across the service sector as well, with the often female and minority workforces there moving from precarious work to no work at all. From 2008 on, employer pressures on collective bargaining for union concessions has been unrelenting. The lack of union representation and/or the weakness of unions have allowed employers in financial difficulty (whether due to the crisis or otherwise) to try to renege on obligations on pensions, severance benefits, overtime pay, and so forth. Because of the gutting of the enforcement of labor standards and regulations by neoliberal policies, employers have had very little to worry about in terms of state sanctions. The hardships this imposes on so many workers, however, together with their outrage at being denied what they see as legitimately theirs, affords unions and workers' centers new grounds for mobilization.

At a time when governments have so openly and massively bailed out the banks and some giant industrial corporations, the necessity for an activist union movement which refuses to grant concessions to employers is obvious. "Anti-concessions campaigns" could also enjoy broad popular appeal. And opposition to union leaders reopening collective agreements to make concessions on work time and wages can encourage more militant workplace tactics, such as plant occupations, and aggressive community mobilizations against companies that use the threat of layoffs or shutdowns to get their way. In reaching out to unorganized sectors where vulnerable workers face abusive employers, "flying squads" of union militants and supporters need to be actively built up as part of an anti-concessions movement. Furthermore, organizing the unorganized has to be a central component of an anti-concessions campaign. It would have to include a campaign for a new legal framework favoring union organizing to overturn neoliberal policies of de-unionization.

It is important not to lose sight of the larger class politics of anti-concessions campaigns. The American state, determined to renew both U.S. and global capitalism, has responded to the crisis in the largest and most radical ways: money dropped from the sky on the financial system, interest rates lowered to zero, and the most significant economic stimulus since the Great Depression. The U.S. state and capitalist classes then had the high-handed audacity to tell the UAW that they must henceforth follow the non-union example of U.S.-based Japanese transplants like Toyota in their collective bargaining. The question that has then faced UAW members, and the North American labor movement more generally, is whether workers can develop the confidence to think as big and as radical as "they"—the American ruling class—are doing in terms of both how workers see the future and what needs to be done to build the capacities to get there.

There is an inevitable logic to concessions: if concessions are simply accepted, more will follow. As pressures continue on the Detroit Three, for example, and with the companies having learned that auto workers will accept cutba cks even in their healthcare benefits, further demands for pension cuts will be next. Since the Japanese transplants have kept their compensation and conditions at their levels in large part to avoid the unionization threat from the UAW, which is now dormant, there has been little to stop them as they cut back on their present levels of pay, benefits, and work conditions. This leads in turn to unionized companies requiring further concessions, not only in auto but in other sectors. Thus anti-concessions campaigns would have to extend beyond the defense of particular plants and workers—the failed strategy of "competitive unionism"—and be framed as a class and community demand.

As a result of long-standing neoliberal policies, public sector workers have also been faced with limits on their union rights, deteriorating working conditions, and a decline in the quality of the public services that they provide. And while the main attacks on workers during the crisis initially came in the private sector, this spread quickly to public sector workers, and persisted even more strongly as the economy showed signs of recovery. Due to the pressures governments faced in light of large budgetary deficits they introduced new cutbacks in services that involved layoffs and the intensification of work, as well as wage and benefit reductions in the public sector. They mobilized popular opinion to back them in this targeting of public sector workers by pointing to the roll back of wages and benefits in the private sector as the new standard that all workers now needed to adhere to on "fairness" grounds. The struggle over state public finances in California is the exemplar of what is likely to spread across North America (with sharp conflicts between public sector workers and governments also unfolding in Ireland, Greece, and Iceland). Business and governments have used the crisis not just to roll back particular gains, but as an opportunity to try and weaken unions as the key working class organization and so more permanently weaken the ability of working people to defend themselves. For these reasons, resisting the attacks on past gains in the public sector is a crucial matter.

But militancy itself won't be enough. Public sector unions and services have been under attack for thirty years now and no effective response has developed during that time. That failure is most evident at this moment: given that the financial crisis has exposed so spectacularly the failure of the market and neoliberal governance, it is not the public sector workers who should be on the defensive. It is absolutely necessary to avoid the notion that the "new reality" means that public sector workers must now accommodate and work more closely with the employer to solve the budgetary problems. This is a dead end: it essentially means unions giving up. The relationships public sector unions need to deepen are not with governments as employers, as that will only further divide working people. New relationships and alliances need to be built with other workers and social movements. For public sector workers, this raises a whole host of questions about overcoming the general denigration of the public sector in favor of the private sector. Unions need to play a leading role in criticizing the bureaucratic shortcomings of public sector employers—governments—to provide a vision of, and mobilize around, a more progressive, egalitarian, and democratic public sector.

It is possible, for example, to envision new kinds of union campaigns linking public sector workers and communities, producers and users, in opposition to neoliberalism. It can also be insisted that responses to the aftermath of the economic slowdown begin with restoring the public sector, since so many years of financial sector-led growth has ended in the current debacle. A number of campaigns—notably some of the anti-privatization struggles around healthcare, universities and municipal services—have had successes across several countries. These community-union alliances have often lacked full union support, even when major campaigns and demonstrations suggest enormous potential. This is, however, also a reflection that social democratic parties have moved to a post-class, post-partisan, and post-campaigning managerial culture. Unions and community groups have been fighting without organizing support at the political level of the forces that these campaigns engage. But whatever the limits, new union and Left organizational capacities, in both connections and political consciousness, keep being built in the process.

The very defeat of the union movement in the advanced capitalist countries at the hands of neoliberalism provides, paradoxically, a third opening. It requires unions to fundamentally assess and transform their own institutions and practices in the struggle for a post-neoliberal—even post-capitalist—order. This is partly about looking at the organizational divisions of unions as they now exist. It is especially about a process that sees unions as empowering workers and contributing to building a different society—social justice unionism.[89]

This entails democratizing the internal practices of unions, expanding education of members, encouraging rank and file activism in leading strategic orientations and struggles, and examining union practices on gender and race, and incorporating a diverse membership into an equally diverse leadership. But the question of union democracy involves more than voting for leaders: it is about empowering the members to collectively effect change. It's therefore about both process and the kind of union that is being built. That is why the potential for union democracy and the level of struggle often seem so closely linked.

At those moments when unions are fighting the status quo, workers receive information and analysis that counters what they get elsewhere. Educationals can come alive. Workers can develop their ability to articulate their cause and strategize. The capacity to organize in the workplace and community is deepened. The confidence that emerges from active participation may spill over into other dimensions of workers' lives and sometimes raises larger questions about democracy in society. These can be powerful and revealing: if we live in a democracy, why do corporations and financiers have so much power over our lives?

In contrast, when unions are only adapting to the status quo, democracy suffers because, from the leadership's perspective, democracy may represent a *problem* rather than an asset. If the leadership is arguing for concessions, it is repeating the arguments of the corporations, not giving workers an independent perspective. If bargaining is reduced to making deals with companies, the members become a nuisance. Educationals on past struggles become counterproductive. Collective Agreements are rushed through without a real chance for consideration. Workers who vote against concessions are told to vote again "until they get it right." Actions that go against union principles cannot be justified, so they must simply be rammed through without reasoned debate. In this context, prospects of an election raising questions about how the union functions, as well as leadership accountability, are seen as a threat, not an opportunity.

The problems go much deeper and involve issues central to *all* unions. What unions face today is rooted in the way North American unions failed to organize themselves in much better economic times to prepare themselves for times like the present. Workers are now suffering for this lack of preparation. While corporations have become more radical and aggressive, the labor movement has become more cautious and defensive. The most important question for the labor movement is to come to grips with those past failures and the need to become as radical as the other side. If we don't develop a vision that fundamentally questions the anti-social logic of capitalism, and build the collective capacities that can challenge corporate power, things won't just stay the same. They are likely to get worse.

These are steps of internal organizational renewal. But it is also necessary to reinsert unions as a central component of wider struggles about work and production. One way is through extending union membership into workplaces even where a majority membership has not been attained, as a means to break through employers' hostility or to amalgamate workers dispersed across small service-sector worksites. Another is to make local labor councils key centers of working class political activism. This should go beyond campaigns for living wages to immigrant workers' rights, economic and even building new forms of working class organization. Organizational renewal is crucial to forging a new anti-neoliberal "common sense" in the day-to-day activities of union members.

If these openings lead to new political struggles that create wider traction across the union movement, a reversal of the way neoliberalism has damaged working class organization will have begun. In such a context, it is possible to envision an outline of an alternative union development model emerging. In collective bargaining, for example, new ways to address wage improvements and employment expansion could be adopted. Solidaristic work policies that radically redistribute work through work-time reduction, overtime caps, and sabbatical and parental leave might be vigorously pursued. Bargaining might set a goal in the form of sharing productivity gains in the form of annual work-time reduction alongside an annual wage improvement. Work-time reduction is indeed essential to expand the capacity for self-management at work and leadership in the community.

And alternative workers' plans for quality, ecologically sustainable production—an imperative, given the need to make a "green" transition to a carbon emissions-neutral energy economy—could begin to build the foundation for expanding workers' control over enterprises. An expansionary fiscal policy to respond to the economic crisis might not only rebuild the public sector, but also be linked to unionization and a longer-term strategy to re-establish a redistributional tax system.

The closing of the gap between international solidarity and social justice movements and the union movement is a fourth opening that needs to become central to union strategy and struggle.[90] The formation of international production networks has partly made this a central issue for collective bargaining. Works councils and campaigns across companies and sectors are a basic mechanism to reduce competition between workers (rather than serve as a mechanism, as works councils have sometimes been, to increase company competitiveness) and to form a capacity to coordinate struggles. There have been examples of these efforts in the steel, auto, and healthcare sectors extending across North America to both Europe and Latin America. One of the more interesting campaigns is the fight against the militantly anti-union Wal-Mart, which has involved a large number of unions in different countries attempting to support union organizing campaigns. But these have often been only consultative and have not explored the potential for concrete union mobilization in support of specific struggles and campaigns. With union movements on the defensive on a national basis from neoliberalism, it is hard to forge new international solidarities. The Wal-Mart case is also revealing from this angle: even the success of union organizing in Canada is linked to unionization drives in the U.S. and the lack of fundamental organizational breakthroughs in North America provide a formidable blockage to international campaigns.

The networks of global production associated with the internationalization of capital also put on the union agenda the ever greater need for international solidarity campaigns. There are a range of these that are pivotal to the global labor movement: the intolerable conditions of Palestinian workers in the Occupied Territories and inside Israel; the continued assaults on unionists in Columbia and the Philippines; the rights of migrant workers to protections parallel to other workers; the rights of workers in countries like Venezuela to nationalize industry and experiment in workers' control; and the need to mobilize labor against the NATO alliance wars of intervention and occupation in the Middle East. These internationalist campaigns require a significant reorientation by union centrals and affiliates, but by breaking with the old chauvinistic and flag-waving practices of American unions in the international arena, they would play an especially important cultural role in union renewal.

Unions and Building Class

To counter the present hostile climate for workers in North America we need a view of unionization that goes beyond adding members to seeing the project as building the working class as a social force. Only such an orientation has the possibility of generating the energy, creativity, commitment, and readiness to undertake risks that have a chance of achieving breakthroughs—institutional risks such as opening the door to unions co-operating to bring new workers into the fold. This would include individual membership in a union that would provide support and services to workers independent of whether or not they have gained collective bargaining rights. This might also be a stepping-stone to winning union recognition from employers.

Suppose, for example, that autoworkers—those laid off and those still working—called for expropriating any plant the companies no longer considered useful to profits, and placed those facilities within a public company with a mandate and plan to convert these plants to socially useful production. The *Wall Street Journal* has reported that even on its own: "The auto-industry meltdown is forcing a transformation among automotive suppliers, which are slowly diversifying into more-promising markets such as medical devices and green energy."[91] But absent a determined national plan that creates the crucial social demand for such conversion, private corporations will only move in this direction sporadically.

An obvious focus of any such plan would be addressing the pressing needs of the environment. The environmental crisis means that, through the rest of this century, we will need to transform everything about how we live, produce, consume, and travel; homes will have to be modified, every machine and piece of factory equipment altered the infrastructure of energy, transportation and cities rebuilt. All this means retaining and expanding manufacturing capacities and jobs. The failed alternative is to passively watch the capacities and jobs continue to fade away.

An alternative vision would not focus on saving the *companies*, but rather on saving the industry's productive *capacities*—the skills of the workers and engineers and the productive capabilities of the equipment. Rather than trying to preserve a falling number of jobs at the car companies—jobs which won't come back—the issue is to reach *beyond* the auto industry to a plan that included all the workers who will not return to auto and looked to *new* jobs that could address other pressing social needs. Rather than depending on corporations driven by profits and on becoming competitive, we'd turn to *democratic planning*. Rather than handing out money to a financial sector at the center of causing the global economic crisis, we'd be talking about nationalizing the banks—not to fix them so they can return to business as usual, but to act as a channel for distributing and investing society's surplus in a democratic way.

In the cases of healthcare and pension even for those unionized workers that have had them for so long, it raises the question of whether the kind of privatized corporate welfare state that the U.S. has developed can continue at all, simply because already corporations cannot live up to their obligations. Unionized workers are learning that if they want social benefits for themselves, they will have to be provided through a universal public system. Winning this in turn rests on mobilizing the working class as a whole. The fundamental importance of a class perspective is equally important when it comes to organizing new workers into unions. As the auto experience has shown, hanging on to unionization in a failing subsection of the industry leads sooner or later to the non-union companies setting the standards for those who are unionized.

The issue goes beyond building a broad alliance to bring about changes in the legal framework confronting unionization. This is crucial but will, in itself, be inadequate. Unless the vision and orientation of those already unionized is transformed, we are left with the limited extent to which unionization in fact represents an increase in independent working class strength and it is unlikely that trying harder will be successful. But how do we get from here to there? How do we build the political capacities—the understanding, confidence and organizational strength—to move on? That unions need to develop closer ties among themselves and link up with other social movements goes without saying. It is clear, as well, that this is not just a matter of bringing together these parts—each with their own limits—but of transforming each of them.

In the case of unions, it is crucial to note that—as central a base as unions are to sustaining progressive change—unions cannot themselves lead the process of radical change. Unions are organizations of workers with different politics that try to create unity around a set of primarily workplace-based ends; the daily administration of contracts and bargaining dominates union life. At their best, unions try to do more and stretch these limits. But the work of broader social change requires a separate organization, one with feet inside the unions but also outside, that identifies its primary task as building toward the possibility of transformative change: coordinating the widest possible popular education; developing grassroots capacities and confidence to analyze, spaces to debate and strategize; and creating new structures through which segmented working classes can participate, socialize, develop unity, and act collectively. These issues point beyond renewal of unions to the need for finally developing a socialist alternative in North America.

CHAPTER SEVEN

ANOTHER WAY OUT OF THE CRISIS? STRATEGIC CONSIDERATIONS FOR THE NORTH AMERICAN LEFT

Over the last quarter century, the Left in most of the developed world has been marginalized as a social force. The culture of possibilities for Left alternatives has correspondingly narrowed. But the crisis that has ended the first decade of the 21st century opens the possibility of, at long last, reversing earlier defeats. The crisis sent neoliberal ideology reeling and delegitimated the call for freer markets as the solution to everything, leaving the right more defensive on economic issues than it has been for a generation. They can no longer get away with calling for the freeing of corporations and financial institutions from regulation to "unleash the creativity of markets" or rejecting out of hand state involvement to address social needs. A world-wide opinion survey in late 2009 found 51 percent calling for regulation and reform of free market capitalism, including nationalization and income distribution, and 23 percent calling for an entirely new system.[92] The desperate need for alternatives is clear enough. The question is whether the Left can develop the capacity to once again be a relevant social actor.

In trying to come to grips with what needs to be done, it is useful to begin by acknowledging the Left's limited capacities at this time. Calls for "re-regulation," with their assumption that states and markets stand in opposition to each other, can further confuse rather than politicize those the Left should be trying to mobilize. As the most recent state interventions make clear, given the current balance of social forces, regulation is about finding a *technical* way to preserve markets in the face of their volatility, not about any fundamental reordering of relative power in society to conform to social needs. Even where the government's involvement has allowed particular capitalists to fail, the content of state intervention has revolved around reconstituting and thereby preserving the power of financial capitalists as a class. This has also involved reinforcing the mechanisms through which the working class has been integrated into financial markets. In the current crisis, the implications of this integration became all too clear: in spite of popular anger over the bailout of Wall Street, there was in the end a general—if reluctant—acceptance of the bailout's necessity to save the financial system on which they had become so dependent.

The strategic question the Left now faces might be stated as follows. All alternatives must begin with people's needs, but can the Left structure its responses so they strengthen popular capacities to think ambitiously and to act independently of the logic of capitalism?

Immediate Demands: The Case for Public Provision

Given the broad impact of the housing crisis and the extent of the delegitimation of the financial sector, it is rather amazing how little direct resistance has occurred—how few community takeovers of foreclosed homes, how few marches, how few spontaneous mass expressions of frustration and anger. Since the financial volcano erupted in the midst of national election campaigns in the U.S. and Canada, it might have been expected that the electoral process would become a catalyst for widespread discussion of dramatic alternatives. But however much the word "change" was repeated, the articulation of radical alternatives was remarkably muted. In Canada, one indicator of the popular political malaise was that voter turnout was the lowest in a hundred years; this could not be said of the U.S. election, yet in putting so much hope in an Obama victory, foreclosure victims waited rather than acted.

Immediate demands and actions in defense of working people's homes and savings, jobs and social programs, should *always* be actively encouraged and supported. But what about demands which go beyond this at such a potentially radicalizing moment? Those that should carry the largest strategic weight today pertain to health care, public pensions and public infrastructure, all of which have the potential to reduce working class dependence on markets and the private sector. Universal health care means not losing your benefits if you lose your job and a consequent lessening of the internalized pressure to strengthen "your" corporation, through concessions if necessary, in order to hang on to your family plan. Public pensions mean less dependence on the returns pension or mutual funds get from growth in the stock market and more security against the increasing trend on the part of corporations to gut union pension plans. Public infrastructure, especially if that includes addressing the environmental crisis, provides jobs and shifts the focus from depending on market incentives to try get private firms to do what is needed to direct public planning and implementation of what is needed.

Thinking about alternatives this way encourages people to look beyond dependence on the profit motive that drives health insurance companies, the managers of institutional funds, or corporations insisting on a favorable business climate to invest (a climate almost always less favorable to public provision). Alternatives that focus on universal rights and collective needs tend to overcome the divisions within the working class and contribute to building class unity and solidarity. Especially poignant in the context of the crisis is the absence of decent public housing. In the 2009 fiscal year, at least $230 billion in U.S. federal expenditures and tax breaks went to support the private housing market; only $10 billion was directed at public housing.[93] Ambitious programs for public housing not only point away from the market as a solution for the poor, but can demonstrate the broader potentials of the public provision of services for everyone. This can be a central element in current rights to the city campaigns, going beyond just building housing stock to raising key democratic demands of worker, resident and community control, affordable and extensive public transportation, access to public spaces and so on.

As for public pensions, it is hardly surprising that business recognized the crisis as an opportunity to escape their private pension commitments. With growth expected to remain sluggish even after the economic crisis ends, and with returns on pension funds investments expected to be low and uncertain—and so requiring more current funding to meet future obligations—worker pensions were identified as supposedly expensive diversion from the real business of the corporations. But more than corporate tactics were involved. As the GM and Chrysler bankruptcies so dramatically highlighted—and business itself now readily admits—private sector pension plans suffer from a definitive contradiction. As an insurance plan, they depend on the survival of specific corporations while the world has changed so that even the viability of the largest corporations can no longer be taken for granted.

Yet crises represent openings for labor as well as business. The difference lies in the extent to which the labor movement, unlike business, has failed (at least so far) to seize the opportunities afforded by this crisis. Unions have accepted dramatic cutbacks in employer funding and pension payouts, including the exclusion of new employees. And faced with inferior pensions or no pensions at all, workers are increasingly looking to individual solutions as they cash in their personal retirement savings plans and work past the age of sixty-five. By letting business off the hook in this way, this has essentially eased the pressures for reform, made business all the more confident in its demands, and left public sector workers increasingly isolated and vulnerable to seeing their pensions cut as well.

In this regard, it is crucial to emphasize that the prospect of a revised universal pension plan set at adequate levels is not a second-best option but the superior alternative. Unlike the private option, it offers universal coverage and thereby provides a foundation for broader solidarity struggles. With pensions not dependent on particular employers, the threat of competition and unemployment would not be a vehicle for other concessions to save pensions (or concessions in pensions themselves so as to not lose them entirely). And the social use of the substantive accumulated pension funds, being in public hands, would be more open—though not automatically so—to democratic pressures. Moving to a public plan will not itself eliminate private finance. Barring a much more radical socialization of finance, pension funds will still continue to operate through financial markets. But a public pension system can limit the dominance of private finance and its scope for profits. Of course, this would leave finance wary about where this might lead.

As for the ever-present question of how provisions of these kinds will be funded, there's no better place to start than making the rich pay—all the more so given the fortunes that were made on the way to the crisis. Making the rich pay should not only focus on progressive income taxation, but on wealth taxes, since it is wealth above all that is so monstrously mal-distributed. But targeting the rich is not enough. The public services that workers depend on require a broad base of taxation, and this is why populist anti-tax sentiments, which reinforce a particular kind of individualism that damages class solidarity and any vision of collective needs, must be challenged.

Yet, redistribution alone won't solve the crisis. Today's bank bailouts and stimulus programs have largely been financed through the sale of government bonds, at a scale last seen in World War II. And given the fear the crisis produced within the business community of investing in anything else, they were only too happy to invest in safe public securities. But the pressures are mounting daily to cut back social programs and lay off public employees and reduce their wages and salaries in order to guarantee the future value of government bonds. Indeed in a capitalist society it is always the implications of state deficits for private finance that ultimately restrain public provision. But rather than constrain public provision, this points to the need to move beyond capitalist finance and the capitalist state.

Democratizing Finance: Nationalize the Banks!

The recent deep crisis of the financial markets should provide an opportunity to press for profound systemic alternatives. It is notable in this respect that over the last century, alongside the various movements that arose to struggle for the vote for working people, there has always been pressure to control the financial system. This reflected a certain common sense that the financial system ought to be accountable to—or even belong to—the people. Even the creation of the Federal Reserve and the nationalization of the Bank of England were presented as matters of responding to popular demands to bring the governments' agents in the financial markets under democratic control. Some of the regulations of the banking system introduced after previous crises were a response to demands from below that people not be fleeced by the bankers and be protected from bank failures, such as through state provided deposit insurance. But the symbiotic nature of the relationship between the state and capitalist finance was not thereby disturbed, and the central banks have continued to act as the organizers of financial capital from inside the state.

There were those on the Left who recognized in the wake of the crisis of the 1970s that the only way to overcome the contradictions of the Keynesian welfare state in a positive manner was to take the whole financial system into public control. We are still paying for the defeat of these ideas. It is now necessary to build on their proposals and make them relevant in the current conjuncture.[94] The scale of the financial meltdown and its consequences shows that a far more ambitious goal than making financial capital more prudent needs to come back on the agenda today. This relates to the issue of immediate demands for collective services and infrastructures that compensate for those that have atrophied under neoliberalism. The vast public expenditures that would be needed for this would soon come up. This is why bringing the banks into the public sector is pivotal to any broader strategy of economic democracy.

This is also why it is so important to raise not merely the regulation of finance but the transformation and democratization of the whole financial system. What is in fact needed is to turn the whole banking system into a public utility so that the distribution of credit and capital would be undertaken in conformity with democratically established priorities, rather than short term profit. Similar considerations arise regarding the kinds of public provisions required to meet the new definitions of basic human needs, including those that come to terms with today's ecological challenges. It is hard to see how anyone can be serious about converting our economy to a sustainable one without understanding that we need a democratic means of planning through new sets of public institutions that would enable us to take collective decisions about allocating resources for what we produce and how and where we produce the things we need to sustain our lives and our relationship to our environment. The reasons trading in carbon offsets as a solution to the climate crisis is a dead end is shown in this financial crisis. It involves depending on the kinds of derivatives market that are so volatile and are so inherently open to financial manipulation and to financial crashes.

If we really take the ecological crisis seriously, then it's not enough to tack on some environmental projects to rebuilding the public infrastructure. Addressing the environment will mean transforming *everything* about what we produce and how we produce it and this can't happen through haphazard market decisions by individual businesses, which are only moved by profits and won't act if they don't know where others will ultimately go. The crisis in auto reinforces this point. A bailout alone, even if it modifies the kinds of vehicles being built, will not overcome the reality of excess capacity. Rather than closing productive facilities, why can't they be converted to produce the new or modified products an environmentally conscious economy will need? As well, given that auto is generally concentrated in certain communities, the issue is not so much a crisis in auto as a crisis in these *communities*. What's needed is a revival plan that includes auto, but also extends to public infrastructure and the range of social services that give a richer meaning to the notion of "community."

What has been most troubling about the current crisis has been the remarkable lack of ambitious vision and program that has characterized the Left's response to it. In the U.S., for instance, one saw the well-meaning but rather mindless populism of those, like Michael Moore, who merely opposed Henry Paulson's bail out of the banks as a rip-off of the taxpayer, saying Wall Street should be left to stew in own juices, and thereby leaving aside what the dependence of people on private financial capital markets actually means: their paychecks are deposited with banks, their pension savings are invested in the stock market, their consumption is reliant on bank credit—and keeping the roof over the heads depends on what happens to mortgage derivative markets.

Many of the proposed reforms often have also displayed an astonishing naïveté about the systemic nature of the relationship between state and capital. This was seen when an otherwise excellent and informative article in the *New Labour Forum* during the crisis founded its case for reform on the claim that "Government is necessary to make business act responsibly. Without it, capitalism becomes anarchy. In the case of the financial industry, government failed to do its job, for two reasons—ideology and influence-peddling."[95] But this misunderstands the nature of the state under capitalism. The state has in fact been very active in promoting the vast expansion of financial markets and facilitating their volatile growth. And as this volatility inevitably led to repeated financial crises, it was also very active in keeping the financial system going from moments of chaos to moments of chaos.

It is this perspective that also perhaps explains why most of the reform proposals advanced were so modest, in spite of the extent of the crisis and the popular outrage. Some of these proposals appeared to be radical only because they went beyond what the Left of the Democratic Party was prepared to call for. One example of this was the proposal advanced by the leading Left voice in financial matters in the U.S., Dean Baker, who at the height of the crisis called for a $2 million limit on Wall Street salaries and a financial transactions tax, along the lines of the Tobin tax. This was a perfect example of thinking inside the box: explicitly endorsing $2 million salaries and the practices of deriving state revenues from the very things that are identified as the problem—very much along the lines of tobacco taxes.[96] Indeed, even broader programs for reform, integrated as they also are with proposals for stringent regulations to prohibit financial imprudence, mostly fail to identify the problem as systemic within capitalism.[97]

And it is precisely because, as we have argued, finance plays such a pivotal role in systemic transformation that nationalization of the banks needs to come on the agenda. We should not be naïve about what this would really have to entail. Many people on the Left seemed to believe that the British government's response to the crisis in the fall of 2008 involved nationalizing the banks. Nothing could be further from the truth as regards the extensive capital the state pumped into British banks. No voting rights came with the preferred shares it bought. The public company, UKFI, that was created to oversee the state's investment in the banks, as its chief executive and chairman immediately made clear in an op-ed article in the *Financial Times*, would "operate on a commercial basis at arm's length" from any government direction or control, seeking mainly to act as to maximize the taxpayers returns on its "investment."[98] Indeed, when the Bank of England reduced interest rates by 1.5 percent and the banks refused to follow, the government was reduced to moral suasion to try to get them to do so. As an outstanding critique of the limits of the UKFI has put it, "it increasingly offered, not so much the nationalization of the banks but the privatization of the Treasury as a new kind of fund manager."[99]

In this context, it fell to a far from radical UK economist, Willem Buiter—a former member of the Bank of England's Monetary Policy Committee and certainly no Marxist—to call (albeit only in his blog) for transforming the whole financial sector into a public utility.

> There is a long-standing argument that there is no real case for private ownership of deposit-taking banking institutions, because these cannot exist safely without a deposit guarantee and/or lender of last resort facilities, that are ultimately underwritten by the taxpayer... The argument that financial intermediation cannot be entrusted to the private sector can now be extended to include the new, transactions-oriented, capital-markets-based forms of

> financial capitalism... From financialization of the economy to the socialization of finance. A small step for the lawyers, a huge step for mankind.[100]

This recalls the demand for "centralization of credit in the hands of the state" that *The Communist Manifesto* put forward. Apparently, you don't need to be a Marxist to have radical aspirations. But some appreciation of Marx's insights may be necessary to recognize that even at a time like the present—when the most important fraction of the capitalist class has been on its heels, demoralized and confused—dispossessing what has been the strongest element of the capitalist class of its base of power is not likely to be matter of just getting lawyers to sign a few documents.

The most important reason for nationalizing the banks is that it would remove the institutional foundation of the power of the financial fraction of the capitalist class, and thus fundamentally shift the balance of power in society. Even if the legal means of doing this are readily available—it's been done in the past as part of the bailouts of both big and small banks—the socialization of finance would mean taking the whole financial sector into the public domain, including near-banks, insurance companies, hedge funds and so on. This would have to include not only capital controls in relation to international finance but also controls over domestic investment, since the point of taking control over finance is to transform the uses to which it is now put. And once we start thinking about how to make banking as a public utility, it quickly becomes clear it would also require much more than this in terms of the democratization of both the broader economy and the state.

In the past, firms were nationalized mainly because they had been bankrupted by the capitalists who ran them, whether they had been banks, railways, or the mines. Despite enormous battles fought by the labor movement to have workers elected to their boards, it was mostly businessman and technocrats and the odd university professor who were appointed board members. Because they were not democratically-run enterprises, politicians like Thatcher were able to get traction amongst working people when they pronounced themselves as against the state. This is why, in making the case for nationalizing the banks today, this has to be put not only in terms of taking capital away from capitalists, but in terms of democratizing the financial system.

Nor should the demand for nationalization be confined to the financial sector. In the context of this crisis it also became clear why the auto industry needs to be nationalized and democratized, with its productive capacities converted to ecologically desirable ends. During the Second World War, the auto industry wasn't producing cars; it had been converted into producing plane fuselages. The enormous skills of the tool and die makers who are losing their jobs today are being wasted as plants are closed. This represents a scandalous loss of the social legacy embodied in the skills of these workers. By taking the whole of the auto industry, including the parts sector, into the public domain, these workers could contribute in crucial ways to the reconversion of the industry and building democratic productive capacities. In turn, these workers, like those in banks as well, would need to come to see themselves as more than just workers but part of a collective project to build a saner, egalitarian, sustainable, democratic, and richer life for all.

From Alternative Policies to Alternative Politics

Attempts to realize even the immediate demands outlined earlier in this chapter would come up against the limits to reform that a capitalist economy imposes, since social programs depend on a growing economy, which in turns depends on the private sector. For social democrats as well as liberals, such contradictions have meant retreating to making more moderate demands. This is a dead end, as was shown by the Democrats' health care reform, where even the competitive public plan (rather than the single payer model) was not realized. The lesson is not to lower expectations but to think bigger and prepare to go further. If democracy is a kind of society and not just a form of government, the economy—which is so fundamental to shaping our lives—will eventually have to be democratized. If domestic or foreign-based capital threatens to move (as they will do earlier rather than later) we must be ready to put capital controls on the agenda. But if we want to channel society's savings to meet social needs—and this is of course the main reason for controlling the social surplus—the controls will have to be on domestic as well as international capital flows. The way forward is not to take one step first and another more radical step later but to find ways of integrating both the immediate demands and the goal of systemic change into the building of new political capacities.

This ultimately raises the question of planning. The negative example of "actually-existing" Communism and the bureaucratic nature of the welfare state must be acknowledged for their effects in making people wary of solutions that leave them dependent on a state they genuinely feel they have no control over and that treats them individually as cogs in the wheel. Though all the technical and democratic issues it involves should not be underestimated, the most important issue is still the question of power, and how to develop democratic capacities to transform the distribution of power in society.

It is in this context of developing individual and collective capacities that the question of limiting work time, which has faded from lists of working class demands, must somehow be revived. Reducing the number of hours people work every day, week, and year as a way of avoiding layoffs and opening up new jobs can be very important in particular sectors and is also a valuable solidaristic principle. But its greatest significance lies in the recognition that effective political participation demands the *time* to do it—the time to read, think, learn, attend meetings and events, debate, take part in strategizing, and engage in organizing others.

The recognition of the importance of all this in movement building goes back to the earliest days of trade unionism, the campaign for women's suffrage, the civil rights movement, and so on. And building on them to go beyond capitalism is not simply about pooling diverse strengths. It is difficult to imagine an alternative politics that can match what we are up against without an organization whose focus is on building new political capacities. How do we build the political capacities—the understanding, confidence and organizational strength—to move on? That labor and other social movements need to develop closer ties among themselves goes without saying. But this is not just a matter of bringing together these parts—each with their own limits—but of transforming each of them. How we do this is what the question of "alternatives" is ultimately about. Crucial to this rebuilding is to get people to think ambitiously again. However deep the crisis, however confused and demoralized the financial elite inside and outside the state, and however widespread the popular outrage against them, this will require hard and committed work by a great many activists.

The impasse of the North American Left that has been cruelly on display over the course of the crisis is reflective of a general waning of socialism and working class politics globally.[101] Working class political organization, in unions and parties, achieved a great deal in the course of the 20th century: leading de-colonization and self-determination struggles; struggling for liberal freedoms and democracy; advancing equality claims for women and racial and sexual minorities; improving wages and benefits; and advancing welfare states and social citizenship. But the social forces that achieved these gains are now quite different. The communist parties have, for good and ill, all but disappeared even in places where they once held power (or they have made their peace with capitalism, as in China); the social democratic parties have politically realigned to chart a so-called Third Way that no longer even poses a reform agenda to neoliberalism; unions are in retreat; and many civil society movements have evolved into professionalized NGOs navigating the grant economy. The central political coordinates for labor movements over the last century—being for or against the Russian Revolution; attempting a vanguard seizure of the existing state apparatus or reforming it piecemeal; conceiving unions as primarily the industrial wing of this or that political party—vanished almost at the same pace as neoliberalism consolidated as the all-encompassing social form of rule.

From both the neoliberal assault on unions and the decline of socialist parties, there slowly emerged the sense across the Left of "starting over" in mapping out the organizational and strategic agendas for social justice and socialism (to the extent that the latter was still seen as a desirable objective at all). This was initially seen in Canada, for instance, with the anti-free trade movement of the late 1980s and the "Days of Action" in the mid-1990s, involving an effort to work through social coalitions apart from political parties, even social democratic ones. In this schema, unions are only one node in a network of oppositional power, and by the end of the 1990s, this strategic outlook became the hallmark of the anti-globalization movement, as a collection of dissident groupings, with unions cautiously making linkages to the movement through so-called Teamster-Turtle alliances.

This "movement of movements" has contained three predominant political clusters.[102] All three were committed, albeit for distinct reasons, to loose horizontal organizational practices. One cluster has encompassed a broad range of primarily policy-oriented if highly militant activists whose main goals have been essentially reformist, whether in calling for corporate responsibility or stopping water privatization, for instance. Another cluster has been an uneasy mix of anarchist, syndicalist, anti-corporate, and indigenous groups who take the view that a combination of spontaneous rebellion and alternative direct practices could directly confront—and also bypass—existing capitalist states, articulating a theoretically-defined autonomist "anti-power" politics which makes the case for changing the world without taking power. A third and smaller cluster has centered around remnants of the revolutionary Marxist Left, and certain strands of Trotskyism in particular, that emphasize global resistance "from below"; believing that a revolutionary conjuncture may be near at hand, they see themselves as the necessary vanguard ingredient of the anti-capitalist movement (they thus saw themselves as the missing party ingredient in the generally anti-party movement of movements). All three clusters have contributed to the revitalized anti-capitalist politics of the World Social Forums, although their national and local offshoots have expressed this mainly in the form of social justice fairs or episodic demonstrations, with little capacity to engage in organized political struggle except through allied political parties, primarily in Latin America.

It is often claimed that the North American anti-globalization movement was cut short when U.S. President Bush began his "war on terror" after September 11, 2001. This requires a sober assessment of the organizational state of the movement and its seeming eclipse over the last years. It seems clear that its network vision of power has not been adequately grounded in working class politics—a renewal of unions, day-to-day community struggles, and the contestation of the class power crystallized in state power and institutions. Nor did they prove capable of sustaining any significant mobilizations as the "long war" across the Middle East that the U.S. unleashed in response to 9/11 unfolded through the last decade. This is especially surprising given the strengths of the global peace movements in fighting the Second Cold War of the 1980s and the first Iraq War. The floundering at both the levels of protest and strategic response to the financial crisis has again illustrated the costs of a lack of grounded organization for unions and the Left as a whole.

It is hard not to conclude that the political thinking and organizational forms that emerged with the anti-globalization movement have proved quite limited in capacity and tentative in strategy. It has not yielded a viable means to contest political hegemony and power in a period of neoliberal globalization and the spread of liberal democratic political institutions. The "national-popular" framing of the issues of the day by the precepts of market organization has not yet been displaced by a socialist version of "common sense." If the anti-globalization movement was quite right to insist on the necessity of moving beyond political frameworks formed in quite different historical moments and national contexts, it has failed to supply the political, ideological, organizational and working-class resources essential to sustain a fight-back over the course of the financial crisis or to build an anti-neoliberal political alliance, never mind build a socialist political force contesting capitalism.

The becalming of even as compelling, vibrant, and engaged a movement as the anti-globalization one has been politically unsettling, but in several places it has encouraged a period of experimentation in new political formations and organizational creativity. This can be seen especially in Latin America, now under the banner of 21st century socialism, but also in significant political realignments and new party formations in Europe, especially in Germany, Greece, Portugal, and France. This can hardly be said to be the case yet in North America.[103] From only a decade ago, having been the site of such robust opposition to neoliberalism and globalization as Seattle and Quebec City, the North American Left appears today to be at an organizational dead-end. It is only beginning to pose the question of how to build anti-neoliberal political alliances and a new politics of a pluralist Left.[104]

This impasse of the Left cannot be addressed by waging in isolation even the most dynamic campaign around a specific issue or community struggle. There have been innumerable of these—Justice for Janitors, housing for the homeless in Toronto, migrant rights marches across the continent, transit workers' strikes in New York—waged in many North American cities. There is a need to shift the current correlation of political forces that is providing the political space for the capitalist classes and the North American states to settle the financial crisis on their terms. There is a need to get beyond the present disorganization and divisions of the Left to create an effective Left alternative.

This means facing up to the imperative of forging a new political instrument for social struggle: to insist on the need to experiment in political parties of a new kind. Marta Harnecker, in her *Rebuilding the Left*, makes the point that "in order to respond to the new challenges set by the twenty-first century we need a political organization which, as it advances a national program which enables broad sectors of society to rally round the same battle standard, also helps these sectors to transform themselves into the active subjects building the new society for which the battle is being waged."[105]

What are the tasks before the Left today? Since there is no shortcut to effective political mobilization that bypasses political education, a primary concern must be to establish an independent infrastructure of socialist media that can contest the daily mainstream interpretation of events, sustain more critical analyses of capitalism, and articulate and discuss alternatives. This involves the sustained building of alternate communications and publications which will now, of course, include the most contemporary forms of media allowed by the internet. But more traditional forms, such a newspapers, pamphlets and magazines remain indispensable for organizing across different workplaces, communities and countries. Educational centers that can cut across current campaigns are absolutely central for developing a deeper and broader understanding of issues, and also for developing the sets of skills that people need to become effective organizers and grounded community leaders.

Second, political activists need to work among the different segments of the working class and gain a deeper understanding of how to build class unity across communities and gender and racial divisions. This involves participating in struggles at the level of community and workplaces as well as in and around trade unions and other popular organizations. It also involves actively trying to develop the potential of workers' centers and community assemblies. The goal should be to create coherent networks of activists, sustained by a socialist media infrastructure, that can advance the kinds of immediate demands and broader socialist alternatives that this chapter has outlined.

Third, a socialist approach to the environment needs urgently to be developed. This is especially so given the drift of so much of the North American ecological movement towards either vulgar market solutions that increasingly overlap with treating the environment as a new site of accumulation (a new environmental-industrial complex), or naïve localist ones that tend to disconnect and internalize local ecologies and communities from wider struggles and political ambitions. An underlying Malthusian determinism often underlies both these cases, in part no doubt, as a well-meaning tactic to scare people into action. But the outcome of seeing the environmental challenge in such end-of-the-world terms is as likely to detract from thinking about the increasingly scarce and costly resource of nature from a class analysis and social justice perspective. This kind of analysis and perspective is also needed to develop an adequate response to the ecological challenges we face due to the practices of global capitalism. The response that is needed will require democratic planning rooted in a different relationship among humans and between humans and nature. This is how a socialist environmental alternative must be framed.

Eco-localism might seem to move the alternative in such an anti-capitalist direction, but it projects the local as an ideal scale for social and economic life and conceives communitarian eco-utopias in a politics that is individualizing and particularizing, evolving under neoliberalism into a practical attempt to only alter individual market behaviors. There is in fact no reason to support, and every reason to oppose, any suggestion that the national and the global are on a scale that is any less human and practical than the local.[106] This is not to deny the importance of the local in anti-neoliberal politics, or the importance of the question of appropriate scale for post-capitalist societies. It is to insist, however, that local socio-ecological struggles cannot be delinked from—and are indeed are always potentially representative of—universal projects of transcending capitalism on a world scale.[107] This is imperative in terms of addressing global issues like climate change, loss of habitats and species, and so forth. But it is also an immediate need to address the needs of daily life, from overwork and hazardous work to the saturation of human bodies with a diet of junk food and endless slurries of pollutants; and the particular burdens of environmental injustices borne by workers, racial minorities, and indigenous people.

All this goes far towards explaining the need for new what Hilary Wainwright has called "parties of a different kind": "Without a process of constantly envisaging and stretching towards such an alternative, there is a danger that the activities and organizations inspired by recent Left movements *would* collapse back, if not into the traditional party system, then into becoming part of an under-resourced, over-exploited voluntary and marginal sector."[108] It can be debated whether in fact this is what has already occurred, and whether the politics of eco-localism, and the brittleness of "red-green" political alliances, have been especially representative of such a "collapse back." But Wainwright's point also contains a contemporary message.

Global social justice movements and world social forums mean little if we cannot challenge local accumulation and sustain campaigns and control in our most immediate political spaces—and thereby ensure that everyday acts of resistance in daily life connect with one another through time, so that they can become the building blocks in the process of collectively helping to envisage and build an organizational alternative. This is most basic element of socialist and ecological renewal.

There is currently a profound unevenness in Left organizational renewal in different parts of the world. In most cases there are only fragile linkages to union movements and only the beginnings of the remaking of working class political organization. It is possible to envision a new dynamic of struggle in a number of workplaces, sectors, and communities unfolding as the crisis imposes new burdens on working class people, that would mobilize the kinds of immediate demands we began this chapter with, whether involving new rights for trade unions, public housing and transportation as part of the right to the city, better public pensions, universal health care, ecologically sustainable infrastructures, and so on. And the barriers that sustaining capitalism puts in the face of winning such demands, are increasingly driving many union, healthcare, community, immigrant-rights and anti-war activists in the direction of anti-capitalist politics.

This offers new possibilities for an emerging political movement that is fully contemporary in terms of its organizational vision as well as in the types of political struggles in which it is rooted. The widespread anti-capitalist sentiments that inform these struggles also make it likely that such a movement will advance socialist alternatives as the only truly democratic route out of the crisis. By sustaining hope about the possibility of developing, even in North America, the organizations and alternatives that might constitute a new socialist project for our time, we can best confront the "crackpot realism" of the current power structures that sustain American capitalism and its state's imperial role in global capitalism.

CHAPTER EIGHT

TEN THESES ON THE CRISIS

The interpretation offered in this book is quite distinct. It is located within the analytical framework of radical political economy, and in particular its lineages in Marx and state theory. We thought it helpful, therefore, to lay out our overall argument succinctly in this concluding chapter by presenting in thesis form our conceptualization of the neoliberal period of capitalism, our reading of the crisis, and the vision and politics behind the strategic alternatives we pose for the North American Left.

I The financial meltdown of 2007–08 has to be understood in terms of the historical dynamics and contradictions of capitalist finance in the second half of the 20th century.

Even though the spheres of finance and production are obviously linked (and in significant ways more so today than ever before), the origins of today's U.S.-based financial crisis are not rooted in a profitability crisis in the sphere of production, as was the case with the crisis of the 1970s, nor directly in the global trade imbalances that have emerged since. Although the growing significance of finance in the major capitalist economies was already strongly registered by the 1960s, it was the role finance played in resolving the economic crisis of the 1970s that explains the central place it came to occupy in the making of global capitalism. The inflation that was the main symptom of this crisis eroded the value of all financial assets but most significant was the fear that U.S. inflation would undermined confidence in the future value of the dollar, both on Wall Street and abroad. To protect the dollar's international role in global capitalism, the U.S. Federal Reserve in the early 1980s used very high interest rates to drive up unemployment, defeat trade union militancy and restrict public welfare expenditures—all of which had come to be seen as the source of the inflation and intractable profitability problems of the previous decade. This laid the basis for global capitalism's finance-led successes in the closing decades of the 20th century, with the lowering of U.S. interest rates and the liquidity poured by the state into the financial system at crucial moments of instability, which was reflected by fewer and milder recessions in comparison with the post-war era. But it was precisely the contradictions in this finance-led capitalism that were at the root of the massive crisis that erupted towards the end of the first decade of the 21st century.

2 The spatial expansion and social deepening of capitalism in the last quarter century could not have occurred without innovations in finance.

The internationalization of American finance allowed for the hedging and spreading of the risks associated with the global integration of investment, production and trade with the dollar rather at its centre. The development of derivative markets provided risk-insurance in a complex global economy without which capital accumulation would otherwise have been significantly restricted. At the same time, more and more working people were drawn into the sphere of finance as debtors, savers, and even investors through private pensions, consumer credit and mortgages for private housing. This became especially important in keeping consumer demand up in a period of wage stagnation and growing economic inequality. The financial sector directly fostered capital accumulation not simply though investments by venture capitalists in high tech, but by developing technical innovations in computerization and information systems. The U.S. dollar and Treasury bonds have served as the key global assets for savings that both earn a return and are tradable, and as the basis for all other calculations of value in the global economy. This predominance of the dollar in global finance reflected and reinforced the global institutional predominance of U.S. financial institutions. It was the basis for the dollar and U.S. bonds acting as a vortex for drawing other countries' savings to American financial markets and instruments, and allowed for the cheap credit that sustained the U.S. as the world's major import and consumer market.

3 The competitive volatility of global finance produced a series of financial crises whose containment required repeated state intervention.

With more funds flowing into the U.S., this increased the competition among lenders and tended to lower interest rates and financial profitability. In response, financial companies looked for new markets but also loaned more relative to their deposits and capital base. This in fact amounted to a vast increase in credit and the effective money supply, which however, given the defeat of labor and the increased corporate ability to fund investments with internal funds, no longer produced price inflation but rather asset inflation in stock and bonds as well as real estate. This was related to the productive strength of particular sectors in the economy, but it led to various financial bubbles based on speculation in and around these sectors. The state stepped in repeatedly to contain the fallout as successive bubbles burst, an action crucial for the confidence of the financial markets—and which encouraged future bubbles to form. The alleged withdrawal of states from the economy amidst the globalization of capitalism was a neoliberal ideological illusion, as states in the developed capitalist countries at the centre of global finance pumped more money into the banks, while they ensured that in the developing countries crises were generally used to impose financial and market discipline on their populations. It was in fact the American state that played the most active role as the imperial guarantor, coordinator and fire-fighter-in-chief for global capitalism.

4 The close linkages between finance and the state was central both to the making of the U.S. housing bubble and to its profound global impact when it burst.

In the context of a highly volatile global financial system, investors gravitated to the safety of U.S. Treasury bonds, despite low U.S. interest rates which reflected a monetary policy designed to prevent a recession in the early 2000s. This intensified the competitive search within global finance for higher yields. The historical safety of mortgages, a very large portion of them backed by the U.S. government, reinforced the public's confidence in perpetually rising home prices. This made housing debt especially attractive to investors who could now borrow funds at low interest and put the money into bundles of mortgages offering much higher returns. A broader stratum of the U.S. working class kept their consumption steady by taking out second mortgages on the bubble-inflated values of their homes, reflecting falling wages and increasingly unequal income distribution resulting from the defeat of labor generally and the restructuring of production and employment. The eventual bursting of the housing bubble necessarily led to an overall decline in U.S. consumer spending, producing effects that the bursting of the stock market bubbles had not. Mortgage-backed securities became difficult to value and to sell in any of the financial markets to which they had spread around the world. Taken together with the impact of the housing crisis on mass consumption, and thus on the U.S. economy's ability to function as the consumer of the rest of the world's goods, illusions that other regions might be able avoid the crisis were quickly dispelled.

5 The crisis revealed the centrality of the American state in the global capitalist economy while multiplying the difficulties entailed in managing it.

The rise of the U.S. dollar in currency markets and the enormous demand for U.S. Treasury bonds as the crisis unfolded reflected the extent to which the world remained on the dollar standard and the American state continued to be regarded as the ultimate guarantor of value. Treasury bonds were in demand because they remained the most stable store of value in a highly volatile capitalist world. Illusions that foreign states were just doing the U.S. a favor by buying Treasury securities may finally be dispelled by this crisis. The American state's central role in terms of global crisis management—from currency swaps that supplied other states with much needed dollars to overseeing policy cooperation among central banks and finance ministries—has also been confirmed in this crisis. Yet despite its very active interventions, the massive amounts of liquidity that states injected to restore levels of lending between banks did not restore the banks' capacity or willingness to lend at anything like previous rates to firms or consumers. Because of the dependence of the economy on the securitized finance—whereby the risk on mortgages, consumer credit and business was sliced, diced, repackaged, and traded around the world—the very crisis in financial markets had limited the impact of fiscal stimulus and lower interest rates in terms of economic revival.

6 **The crisis vividly demonstrated one of Marx's great insights in *The Communist Manifesto*: while capitalism is international in substance, its reproduction remains national in form.**

Whatever the attention paid to international meetings like the G20, all the crucial interventions—economic stimulus, financial bailouts and new regulations—have occurred at the level of individual states. Whereas national reactions to the Great Depression of the 1930s fragmented capitalism, the current responses have not interrupted open trade and the free flow of capital. This is primarily a matter of individual states continuing to take responsibility within their borders for sustaining the essentials of international accumulation, reflecting the underlying structural integration of 21st century capitalism: the close connections and common world-views among key state actors, especially those in central banks and departments of finance; and, above all, the interest and dependence all other states within global capitalism have on the overarching managerial and coordinating role of the American state within that system. This has important implications in terms of thinking strategically about how to respond to the crisis. Alternatives which stress the need for social movements to develop their global network capacities to match the global capitalist forces they confront may miss the crucial importance of first establishing a solid base at home. Absent such a base and the kinds of capacities that can challenge and transform their own states, internationalist sensibilities cannot translate into an effective internationalism. Even beyond the issue of alternative policies, where the national still clearly outweighs the international, this is crucially important in relation to an alternative *politics*.

7 **Looking for alternatives in a return to the good-old pre-neoliberal days misunderstands the connection between then and now, and ignores the extent to which the working classes have been integrated into financial markets.**

Neoliberalism was a response to the *unsustainability* of the earlier period for capitalism. The crisis of the 1970s was rooted in worker resistance to corporate attempts to restore their productivity at the expense of wages and working conditions, which led corporations to slow down their investment and threaten to shift capital abroad. To go back to that earlier period would therefore only reintroduce the previous conflict: whether corporate power would be restored to solve the crisis, or whether a fight could be made for a democratic alternative. After the 1970s, a long period of low wages pushed workers more and more to rely on credit as the form through which they were able to maintain their standard of living. As well, they looked to a rising stock market to boost their pension funds, and those with homes cheered rising house prices because the increase in their wealth reduced the need for savings and so allowed greater consumption. This further fragmented the working class and undermined its cohesion as an independent social force. While the struggle for wages and public benefits depended on and built class solidarity, looking to credit (and lower taxes) to sustain their private lives led to an atrophy of collective capacities. In the current crisis, the implications of that relationship to financial markets became all too clear: in spite of popular anger over bank bailouts, there was in the end a general—if reluctant—acceptance of the necessity to "save the system" they had become dependent on.

8 Alternatives must begin with people's immediate material needs, but must at the same time be oriented to strengthening popular capacities to act independently of the logic of capitalism.

Any forms of resistance in defense of working people's homes or savings, jobs or social programs, should obviously be actively encouraged and supported. More general demands—like the expansion of health care to everyone and to include dental care and drugs, the development of an adequate public pension system for everyone, democratic influence over the kind of public infrastructure that is built so that we get more public housing and public transportation—address both popular concerns and carry a broader strategic weight. They reduce working class dependence on their employers and markets for their security, facilitate class solidarity because of their focus on universal rights and collective needs, and demonstrate the broader potentials of the public provision of services, such as affordable housing that includes a new sense of community and relationship to the surrounding city. Local resistance needs to be connected to this; its success is both dependent on and a condition for mobilizing around larger national issues. The triad of immediate resistance, developing policies for broader popular mobilization, and raising the "big" questions such as democratic planning and nationalizing the banks, are not to be understood as stages of activity. The point is not to take one step first and another more radical step later but to find ways of trying struggles that integrate all three simultaneously.

9 **Since democracy is not just a form of government but also a kind of society, then the economy—so fundamental to shaping our lives—will eventually have to be democratized.** General calls for "re-regulation" of financial markets falsely assume that states and markets, or financial power and state power, stand in opposition to each other. This can confuse rather than politicize progressive constituencies. It is highly significant that the last time the nationalization of the banks was seriously raised, at least in the advanced capitalist countries, was in response to the 1970s crisis by those elements on the Left who recognized that the only way to overcome the contradictions of the Keynesian welfare state in a positive manner was to take the financial system into public control. Since even conservatives flirted with some form of bank nationalization through the crisis, it is very important to contrast temporary nationalization with the fundamental democratic demand for turning the whole financial system into a public utility that allocates national savings on an entirely different basis than governs banking and investment today. This would allow for the distribution of credit and capital to finally be undertaken in conformity with democratically established criteria, and would thus involve not only capital controls in relation to international finance but also controls over domestic investment, since the point of taking control over finance is to transform the uses to which it is now put. The call for nationalization of the banks therefore provides an opening for advancing broader strategies that begin to take up the need for systemic alternatives to the intractable problems of contemporary capitalism. We need to put on the public agenda the need to change our economic and political institutions so as to allow for democratic planning to collectively decide how and where we produce what we need to sustain our lives and our relationship to our environment.

10 The severity of the global economic crisis once again exposed how states are enveloped in capitalism's irrationalities and the need for building new movements and parties to transcend capitalist markets and states.

Even as they tried to stimulate the economy, states were impelled to lay off public sector workers or cut back their pay, and to demand that bailed-out companies do the same. And while blaming volatile derivatives market for causing the crisis, states promoted derivatives trading in carbon credits as a solution to the climate crisis. In the context of such readily visible irrationalities, a strong case can be made that—to really save jobs and the communities that depend on them in a way that converts production to ecologically sustainable priorities during the course of this crisis—we need to break with the logic of capitalist markets rather than use state institutions to reinforce them. However deep the crisis, however confused and demoralized are capitalist elites both inside and outside the state, and however widespread the popular outrage against them, making the case for such a broader democratization will certainly require hard and committed work by a great many activists. They will need to put their minds not only to demanding immediate reforms but how to finally make a genuine democracy that transcends the capitalist economy and state. To clarify that *this* is on the agenda is an essential precondition for building out of this crisis the new movements and parties that are needed to make such a genuine democracy a real possibility.

SUGGESTED READINGS

American Capitalism

There are numerous books, some more classic and some more current, that provide a foundation for a more critical understanding of American capitalism.

Baran, Paul and Paul Sweezy. *Monopoly Capital*. New York: Monthly Review Press, 1966.

Carroll, William. *Corporate Power in a Globalizing World*. Toronto: Oxford University Press, 2004.

Davis, Mike. *Prisoners of the American Dream*. London: Verso, 1986.

Dumenil, Gerard and Dominique Levy. *Capital Resurgent: Roots of the Neoliberal Revolution*. Cambridge: Harvard University Press, 2004.

Gindin, Sam and Leo Panitch. *Global Capitalism and American Empire*. London: Merlin, 2004

Glyn, Andrew. *Capitalism Unleashed: Finance, Globalization and Welfare*. Oxford: Oxford University Press 2007.

Piven, Frances. *The War at Home*. New York: New Press, 2004.

Financialization

A number of recent studies provide important insights into neoliberalism and financialization, which lay the basis for an alternate understanding of money and finance in capitalism.

Altvater, Elmar. *The Future of the Market*. London: Verso, 1993.

Brenner, Robert. *The Boom and the Bubble*. New York: Verso, 2002.

Bryan, Dick. *Capitalism with Derivatives*. New York: Palgrave, 2006.

Harvey, David. *A Brief History of Neoliberalism*. New York: Oxford University Press, 2005.

Henwood, Doug. *Wall Street*. New York: Verso, 1998.

Lapavitsas, Costas. *Social Foundations of Markets, Money and Credit*. London: Routledge, 2003.

Panitch, Leo and Martijn Konings. *American Empire and the Political Economy of Global Finance*. New York, Palgrave, 2009

Soederberg, Susanne. *Corporate Power and Ownership in Contemporary Capitalism*. London: Routledge, 2009.

Left Renewal

Discussions of the pressing issues raised by the need for a new anti-capitalist politics have been advanced by some key texts addressing the challenges of Left renewal in terms of unions and parties of a new kind.

Aronowitz, Stanley. *Left Turn*. Boulder: Paradigm, 2006.
Browne, Jaron, Marisa Franco, Jason Negron-Gonzales, and Steve Williams. *Towards Land, Work & Power: Charting a Path of Resistance to US-Led Imperialism*. San Francisco: Unite to Fight Press, 2005.
Fletcher, Bill and Fernando Gapasin. *Solidarity Divided*. Berkeley: University of California Press, 2008.
Harnecker, Marta. *Rebuilding the Left*. New York: Zed Books, 2007.
Holmstrom, Nancy ed., *The Socialist Feminist Project*. New York: Monthly Review Press, 2002.
Huws, Ursula. *The Making of a Cybertariat*. New York: Monthly Review Press, 2003.
McNally, David. *Another World is Possible*. Winnipeg: Arbeiter Ring, 2006.

Socialist Alternatives

The considerable fresh thinking the Left has exhibited over the last two decades has been exemplified in a number of important books on what some of the features of a democratic socialist alternative might look like.

Albert, Michael. *Parecon: Life After Capitalism*. London: Verso, 2003.
Devine, Pat. *Democracy and Economic Planning*. Boulder: Westview Press, 1988.
Hahnel, Robin. *Economic Justice and Democracy*. New York: Routledge, 2005.
Lebowitz, Michael. *Build it Now*. New York: Monthly Review Press, 2006.
Panitch, Leo. *Renewing Socialism*. London: Merlin Press, 2008.
Wainwright, Hilary. *Reclaim the State: Experiments in Popular Democracy*. New York: Seagull Books, 2009.

Journals

A number of publications of the Left are quite essential for keeping up with ongoing assessments and debates about North American capitalism and Left alternatives. The journal which all three authors are most closely associated with that has been especially important for the analysis presented here is the *Socialist Register* (http://socialistregister.com).

Against the Current, http://www.solidarity-us.org/atc.
Canadian Dimension, http://canadiandimension.com/.
Capitalism Nature Socialism, http://www.cnsjournal.org.
Dollars and Sense, http://www.dollarsandsense.org/.
Labor Notes, http://www.labornotes.org/.
Left Business Observer, http://www.leftbusinessobserver.com/.
Monthly Review, http://www.monthlyreview.org/.
Studies in Political Economy: A Socialist Review, http://spe.libraryutoronto.ca.
Work Organization Labour & Globalization, http://analyticapublications.co.uk.

NOTES

1 Thomas Edsall, "Alan Greenspan: The Oracle or the Master of Disaster?" http://www.huffingtonpost.com/2009/02/19/alan-greenspan-the-oracle_n_168168.html.

2 Ben S Bernanke, "Four Questions about the Financial Crisis," speech at Morehouse College, April 14, 2009, http://www.federalreserve.gov/newsevents/speech/bernanke20090414a.htm.

3 Paul Mason, *Meltdown: The End of the Age of Greed* (London: Verso, 2009) vii, x.

4 Rick Wolff has particularly analyzed this aspect of the crisis on MRZINE. See, for example, "Class War," September 16, 2009; "Capitalism's Crisis Through a Marxian Lens," December 14, 2008.

5 The theme of capitalist decay can in fact be dated back to Karl Kautsky's drafting of *The Erfurt Programme* in the late 19th century and V.I. Lenin's *Imperialism: The Highest Stage of Capitalism* at the beginning of the 20th century. It was a theme then applied to American capitalism in the writings of Paul Baran and Paul Sweezy, *Monopoly Capital* (New York: Monthly Review Press, 1966) and Ernest Mandel, *Marxist Economic Theory* (London: Merlin Press, 1962).

6 Most notably in this respect have been Michael Perelman, *The Pathology of the U.S. Economy* (1993); Giovanni Arrighi's *The Long Twentieth Century* (1994); David Harvey's *The New Imperialism* (2003): Robert Pollin, *Contours of Descent* (2003), and Robert Brenner, *The Economics of Global Turbulence* (2006).

7 A debate particularly carried on in the pages of *The Nation* and *American Prospect* over the last two years. More critical stances can be found in the pages of *Monthly Review*, *Against the Current* and *International Socialist Review*.

8 The foremost examples of this contention being: Sam Bowles, David Gordon and Thomas Weisskopf, *After the Wasteland: A Democratic Economy for the Year 2000* (Armonk: M.E. Sharpe, 1990); Robert Reich, *The Work of Nations* (New York: Knopf, 1991). An updated version of this theme is Joseph Stiglitz, *Freefall: America, Free Markets, and the Sinking of the World Economy* (New York: Norton, 2009).

9 Krishna Guha, "Ten Years of Cuts and Tax Rises Lie Ahead, IMF Says," *Financial Times*, November 4, 2009.

10 These struggles have been covered at the following websites: Reclaiming Spaces at www.reclaiming-spaces.org/crisis/archives/category/housing-the-crisis; Socialist Project at www.socialistproject.ca; and Labor Notes at www.labornotes.org.

11 *The Lexus and the Olive Tree* (New York: Anchor Books, 2000), 86–7.

12 Ibid., 86–7.

13 The best of these is Kevin Phillips, *Bad Money* (New York: Penguin, 2009).

14 For defenses see: Daniel Yergin, "A Crisis in Search of a Narrative," *Financial Times*, October 21, 2009; Institute of International Finance, *Reform in the*

Financial Services Industry: Strengthening Practices for a More Stable System (Washington: IIF, 2009). For a critique see: James Crotty, "Structural Causes of the Global Financial Crisis," *Cambridge Journal of Economics* 33 (2009).

15 Karl Marx, *The Grundrisse* (Middlesex: Penguin, 1973), 623.

16 Irving Fisher, "The Debt-Deflation Theory of Great Depressions," *Econometrica* 1 (October 1933).

17 Niall Ferguson, *Too Big to Live: Why We Must Stamp Out State Monopoly Capitalism* (Surrey: Centre for Policy Studies, 2009), 16.

18 See Hyman Minsky's *Stabilizing an Unstable Economy* (New York: McGraw Hill, 1986) and Doug Henwood, *Wall Street* (New York: Verso, 1997).

19 Paul Krugman, *The Return of Depression Economics and the Crisis of 2008* (New York: W.W. Norton, 2009); Joseph Stiglitz, *Making Globalization Work* (New York: W.W. Norton, 2007).

20 Paul Mason, *Meltdown* (London: Verso, 2009); Robert Wade, "From Global Imbalances to Global Reorganizations," *Cambridge Journal of Economics* 33 (2009).

21 J.B. Foster and Fred Magdoff, *The Great Financial Crisis* (New York: Monthly Review Press, 2009); Andrew Glyn, *Capitalism Unleashed: Finance, Globalization and Welfare* (Oxford: Oxford University Press, 2007); Giovanni Arrighi, *Adam Smith in Beijing* (London: Verso, 2007); Robert Brenner, *The Boom and Bubble* (London: Verso, 2002).

22 Peter Gowan, "Crisis in the Heartland," *New Left Review* 55 (2009); David Harvey, *Limits to Capital* (Chicago: University of Chicago Press, 1982), Chapters 9–10.

23 Karl Marx and Friedrich Engels, *The Communist Manifesto* (1848) (London: Verso, 1998), 41–2.

24 Karl Marx, *Capital*, vol. 3 (1894) (London: Penguin, 1981), 357.

25 Karl Marx, *Capital*, vol. 1(1867) (New York: International Publishers, 1967), 592.

26 Leo Panitch and Sam Gindin, "Superintending Global Capital," *New Left Review* 35 (2005); Simon Clarke, "Class Struggle and Global Overaccumulation" in *Phases of Capitalist Development*, ed. Robert Albritton, et al. (New York: Palgrave, 2001).

27 Among the various significant analyses of the financial crisis of 2007–09, see L. Panitch et al., "The Political Economy of the Subprime Crisis" in *American Empire and the Political Economy of Global Finance*, 2nd ed., eds. Panitch and Martijn Konings (London: Palgrave, 2009); David McNally, "From Financial Crisis to World Slump," *Historical Materialism* 17 no. 2 (2009); Robin Blackburn, "The Subprime Crisis," *New Left Review* 50 (2008); Julie Guard and Wayne Antony, eds., *Bankruptcies and Bailouts* (Halifax: Fernwood Books, 2009); Graham Turner, *The Credit Crunch* (London: Pluto, 2008).

28 Robert Rubin and Jacob Weisberg, *In an Uncertain World: Tough Choices from Washington to Wall Street* (New York, Random House: 2003), 297.

29 Willem Buiter, "The Fed as the Market Maker of Last Resort: Better Late Than Never," *Financial Times*, March 12, 2008.

30 Peter Baker, "A Professor and a Banker Bury Old Dogma on Markets," *New York Times*, Sept. 20, 2008, A1.

31 Ron Chernow, *The House of Morgan* (New York: Simon & Schuster, 1990), 121.

32 Chernow, 123–5.
33 Ibid., 128.
34 Murray N. Rothbard, "The Origins of the Federal Reserve," *The Quarterly Journal of Austrian Economics* 2 no. 3 (Fall 1999). See also J. Livingston, *Origins of the Federal Reserve System: Money, Class and Corporate Capitalism*, 1890–1913 (Ithaca: Cornell University Press, 1986.)
35 Cited in John J. Broesamle, *William Gibbs McAdoo: A Passion for Change, 1863–1917* (Port Washington, N.Y: Kennikat Press, 1973), 129.
36 Giovanni Arrighi, *The Long Twentieth Century* (London: Verso, 1994), 272.
37 Michael Moran, *The Politics of the Financial Services Revolution* (New York: Macmillan, 1991), 29.
38 Alan Brinkley, *The End of Reform: New Deal Liberalism in Recession and War* (New York: Alfred A. Knopf, 1995), 89–90.
39 Gerald A. Epstein and Juliet B. Shor, "The Federal Reserve-Treasury Accord and the Construction of the Postwar Monetary Regime in the United States," *Social Concept* (1995), 27. See also Edwin Dickens, "US Monetary Policy in the 1950s: A Radical Political Economy Approach," *Review of Radical Political Economics* 27 no. 4 (1995), and his "Bank Influence and the Failure of US Monetary Policy during the 1953–54 Recession," *International review of Applied Economics* 12 no. 2 (1998).
40 During the War the Fed "had run the market for government securities with an iron fist" in terms of controlling the prices that were set by the Treasury for its bonds, the Fed now took up the position long advocated by University of Chicago economists and set to work successfully organizing Wall Street's bond dealers into a self-governing association that would ensure they had "sufficient depth and breadth" to make "a free market in government securities," and thus allow market forces to determine bond prices. The Fed's Open Market Committee would then only intervene by "leaning against the wind" to correct "a disorderly situation" through buying and selling Treasury bonds (Robert Herzel and Ralph F. Leach, "After the Accord: Reminiscences on the Birth of the Modern Fed" in Federal Reserve Bank of Richmond, *Economic Quarterly* 87 no.1 [Winter 2001]: 57–63.)
41 See *Leo Melamed on the Markets: Twenty Years of Financial History as Seen by the Man Who Revolutionized the Markets* (New York: Wiley, 1992), esp. pp. 43, 77–8. See also Dick Bryan and Michael Rafferty, *Capitalism with Derivatives. A Political Economy of Financial Derivatives, Capital and Class* (London, Palgrave, 2006).
42 Leo Panitch, "A Socialist Alternative to Unemployment," *Canadian Dimension* 20 no. 1 (March 1986).
43 Angus Maddison, *The World Economy: A Millennial Perspective* (Paris: OECD, 2001), 265.
44 Karen Weaver, "US Asset-Backed Securities Market: Review and Outlook," in Deutschebank, *Global Securitization and Structured Finance*, 2008.
45 National Association of Realtors, S&P/Case-Shiller Home Price Index.
46 Thomas Ferguson and Robert Johnson, "Too Big To Bail: The 'Paulson Put,' Presidential Politics, and the Global Financial Meltdown, Part I: From Shadow Financial System to Shadow Bailout," *International Journal of Political Economy* 38 no. 1 (2009).

47 Alan Greenspan, "Consumer Finance," Federal Reserve Fourth Annual Communities Affairs Research Conference, Washington, D.C., April 8, 2005.

48 Ibid.

49 Robert Rubin, *In an Uncertain World: Tough Choices from Wall Street to Washington* (New York: Random House, 2003).

50 Philip Rucker and Joe Stephens, "Top Economics Aide Discloses Income: Summers Earned Salary From Hedge Fund, Speaking Fees From Wall St. Firms" *Washington Post*, April 4, 2009.

51 Robert G. Gordon, "'The Ideal and the Actual in the Law': Fantasies and Practices of New York City Lawyers, 1870–1910," in *The New High Priests: Lawyers in Post-Civil War America* by Gerald W. Gewalt (Westport, CT: Greenwood Press, 1984), 53, 58, 65–6.

52 Michael Moran, *The Politics of the Financial Services Revolution* (London: Macmillan, 1991), 13.

53 U.S. Bureau of the Census, Historical Income Tables, http://www.census.gov/hhes/www/income/histinc/incpertoc.html.

54 S. Kirchhoff and J. Keen, "Minorities Hit Hard by Rising Costs of Subprime Loans," *USA Today*, April 25, 2007.

55 Statistical Abstracts of the U.S., 2005–2007.

56 See Karen Weaver, "US Asset-Backed Securities Market: Review and Outlook," in Deutschebank, *Global Securitisation and Structured Finance*, 2008, http://www.globalsecuritisation.com/08_GBP/GBP_GSSF08_018_021_DB_US_ABS.pdf

57 See Ben Bernanke, *Essays on the Great Depression* (Princeton, NJ: Princeton University Press, 2000).

58 D. Solomon, "Questions for Paul O'Neill, Market Leader," *New York Times*, March 30, 2008.

59 C. Mollenkamp et al., "Rescue Readied by Banks is Bet to Spur Markets," *Wall Street Journal*, October 15, 2007.

60 German Finance Minister Peer Sienbrück in Bertrand Benoit's "US 'will lose financial superpower status,'" *Financial Times*, September 25, 2008.

61 Martin Wolf, 'Why a Successful US Bank Rescue is Still So Far Away," *Financial Times*, March 24, 2009.

62 Philip Hampton and John Kingman, "Mandate to Protect Taxpayers' Investment," *Financial Times*, November 13, 2008.

63 Ralph Miliband, *The State in Capitalist Society* (1969) (London, Merlin Press: 2009), 198.

64 Ibid., 73.

65 David Stout, "Paulson Gives Way on CEO Pay," *New York Times*, September 24, 2008.

66 Simon Bowers, "Wall Street Man," *The Guardian*, September 26, 2008.

67 Quoted in Stout, "Paulson Gives Way," emphasis added.

68 Quoted in Andrew Ward, "Obama Urges Restraint Over Bonus Penalties," *Financial Times*, March 24, 2009, emphasis added.

69 Anna Fifield, "Obama in Tough Talk to 'Fat Cat' Bankers," *Financial Times*, December 15, 2009, 18.

70 See especially the report of a steering committee the Group of Thirty chaired by Paul Volcker, *Financial Reform: A Framework for Financial Stability*, Washington, D.C., January 15, 2009.

71 Tom Braithwaite and Krishna Guha, "Banks Face Revolutionary Reform" *Financial Times*, January 21 2010.

72 According to *Time*, October 6, 1961, what Wilson actually said during the confirmation hearings to make him Secretary of Defense under Eisenhower in 1952, was "For years I thought that what was good for our country was good for General Motors, and vice versa," http://www.time.com/time/magazine/article/0,9171,827790,00.html#ixzz0aBqBo1MJ.

73 http://money.cnn.com/magazines/fortune/fortune500_archive/full/2000/.

74 See the ResCap web-site at https://www.gmacrfc.com/about/history.asp.

75 See Nicole Aschoff's very important thesis, *Globalization and Capital Mobility in the Automobile Industry*, (Baltimore: John Hopkins University, 2009).

76 Julie Froud, Sukhdev Johal, Adam Leaver, and Karel Williams, *Financialization and Strategy: Narrative and Numbers* (London: Routledge, 2006).

77 The American state's direct intervention, through the loan conditions, against the wages, benefits, and working conditions of autoworkers was remarkable – and even more so in light of the treatment of Wall Street and those who were so implicated in causing the crisis. The GM loan conditions demanded that "By no later than February 17, 2009, the Company shall submit... [a] term sheet signed on behalf of the Company and the leadership of each major U.S. labor organization [essentially the UAW] that represents the employees" that – over and above the elimination of any layoff benefits above customary severance pay, something the union had already conceded – there be a reduction in workers' wages, benefits and working conditions to match "no later than December 31, 2009" levels that are "competitive with the average as certified by the Secretary of Labor" at the U.S. operations of Nissan, Toyota, and Honda. As well, the union had to accept that at least half of each company's obligations to the union administered health care plan would now include company stock (the full terms are available at www.ustreas.gov/press/rcleases/hp1333.htm).

78 Herman Rosenfeld, "Crisis in the North American Auto Industry, *Monthly Review* (June 2009). Rosenfeld's analysis parallels, but goes into more current detail, on the crisis in auto; see especially the excellent section on alternatives. For further analysis on the auto industry see the Socialist Project labor page and *Bullets* (www.socialistproject.ca); *Labor Notes* (www.labornotes.org/); and Gregg Shotwell's outstanding articles on the SOS website, *Live Bait & Ammo* (www.soldiersofsolidarity.com/files/livebaitammo/livebaitammo.html)

79 The Big Three were ready to concede this low-profit end of the market, largely because any success here was seen as cutting into the large market in the U.S. for their own higher-profit larger vehicles. Toyota later also followed this same capitalist logic; Toyota's 84-year old patriarch recently scolded the company president for "being so anxious to boost sales and profits that he'd let Toyota emulate the now bankrupt General Motors and Chrysler [in] becoming addicted to big, expensive cars and trucks" ("Toyoda Asks How Many Times Toyota Errs Emulating GM," *Bloomberg*, June 22, 2009). More generally, Toyota's reputation as a model manufacturer has dramatically fallen: see "Toyota at Crossroads, Survey Warns," *Ward's Automotive News*, November

30, 2009 and "Toyota Slips Up," *Economist* (editorial), December 12, 2008. As for Toyota's Prius, this represented less a commitment to the environment than an appreciation of the beneficial image of being environmentally conscious. Before the crisis hit, Toyota was selling 150,000 Prius cars in the U.S. but also building a new $1.3-billion plant in Texas to produce 200,000 heavy-duty Tundra pick-ups for personal as well as business use so as to cash in on the larger profits generated by such vehicles (some ten-fold in levels of profits in comparison to that of the Prius). As it turned out, Toyota had to mothball the plant when, like GM, it confronted the sudden collapse of the pick-up truck market ("Toyota's Prius May not be the 'Savior' for Earnings Recovery," *Bloomberg*, June 10, 2009. "Toyota Falters in Booming China," *China Automotive Movement News*, May 9, 2009).

80 Ironically, by the time of the GM and Chrysler bankruptcies, studies were confirming that the quality gap with the Japanese transplants had become "statistically insignificant" and that the productivity gap was "nearly erased." What remained, however, was the continuing perception of that gap, GM's inability to adjust in the face of the economic collapse, and Detroit's well-publicized cost disadvantage relative to the transplants. Ironically, by the time of the GM and Chrysler bankruptcies, studies were confirming that the quality gap with the Japanese transplants had become "statistically insignificant" and that the productivity gap was "nearly erased" (*Harbor Report*, June 5, 2008).

81 This is more generally confirmed in a report by the President's Economic Council of Advisors, which notes that once healthcare is excluded, the growth in overall worker compensation is surprisingly flat. See "The Economic Case for Healthcare Reform," Council of Economic Advisors, June 2, 2009, http://www.whitehouse.gov/administration/eop/cea/TheEconomicCaseforHealthCareReform/.

82 Though Canada's healthcare system avoided this disadvantage, because the Canadian operations were so integrated into the higher cost U.S. operations, the U.S. problem was also a Canadian problem.

83 See Aschoff, *Globalization and Capital Mobility in the Automobile Industry*.

84 Monthly Labor Review, U.S. Department of Labor, February 2008, http://www.bls.gov/opub/mlr/2008/02/contents.htm.

85 Kim Moody, *Workers in a Lean World* (London: Verso, 1997); Greg Albo and Dan Crow, "Under Pressure: The Impasses of the North American Labour Movement" in *Politics in North America: Redefining Continental Relations*, eds. Yasmeen Abu-Laban, Radha Jhappan and Francois Rocher (Peterborough: Broadview Press, 2008).

86 Leo Panitch and Donald Swartz, *From Consent to Coercion: The Assault on Trade Union Freedoms* (Aurora: Garamond, 2003).

87 Kim Moody, "Are U.S. Unions Ready for a Challenge of a New Period?" *New Politics* 12 no. 3 (2009): 30.

88 Rick Fantasia and Kim Voss, *Hard Work: Remaking the American Labor Movement* (Berkeley: University of California Press, 2004); Pradeep Kumar and Chris Schenk, eds. *Paths to Union Renewal* (Toronto: Garamond, 2006).

89 Bill Fletcher and Fernando Gapasin, *Solidarity Divided: The Crisis in Organized Labor and a New Path Toward Social Justice* (Berkeley: University of California Press, 2008).

90 Peter Waterman, *Globalization, Social Movements, and the New Internationalisms* (New York: Continuum, 2001); Leo Panitch and Colin Leys, eds., *Socialist Register: Working Classes, Global Realities* (London: Merlin Press, 2001).

91 Timothy Aeppel, "Auto Suppliers Attempt Reinvention," *Wall Street Journal,* June 15, 2009, B1.

92 Alan Beattie, "Survey Finds a World Skeptical of Free Markets," *Financial Times,* November 23, 2009.

93 Doug Henwood, "Federally Subsidized Dreaming," *Left Business Observer* no.123, November 25, 2009.

94 Still worth reading today is Richard Minns, *Take over the City: The Case for Public Ownership of Financial Institutions* (London: Pluto, 1982).

95 John Atlas, Peter Dreier, and Gregory Squires, "Foreclosing on the Free Market: How to Remedy the Subprime Catastrophe," *New Labour Forum* (Fall 2008).

96 Dean Baker, "Big Banks Go Bust: Time to Reform Wall Street," *truthout,* September 15, 2008, http://www.truthout.org/article/big-banks-go-bust-time-reform-wall-street.

97 This even applies to the admirably broad agenda advanced by a group of radical U.S. political economists in *A Progressive Program for Economic Recovery and Financial Reconstruction,* http://www.peri.umass.edu/fileadmin/pdf/other_publication_types/PERI_SCEPA_statementJan27.pdf

98 Philip Hampton and John Kingman, "A Precise Mandate to Protect Taxpayers' Interests," *Financial Times,* November 14, 2008.

99 Julie Froud, Michael Moran, Adriana Nilsson, and Karel Williams, "Wasting a crisis? Democracy and Markets in Britain after 2007," forthcoming *Political Quarterly,* 2010.

100 Willem Buiter, "The End of American Capitalism as We Knew It," Financial Times Maverecon Blog, September 17, 2008, http://blogs.ft.com/maverecon/2008/09/the-end-of-american-capitalism-as-we-knew-it/.

101 Leo Panitch and Colin Leys, eds., *Socialist Register: Working Classes, Global Realities* (London: Merlin Press, 2001); Donald Sassoon, *One Hundred Years of Socialism* (New York: The New Press, 1996).

102 Alex Callinicos, *An Anti-Capitalist Manifesto* (Oxford: Polity, 2003); William Fisher and Thomas Ponniah, eds., *Another World is Possible* (New York: Zed Books, 2003); Michael Hardt and Antonio Negri, *Multitude* (New York: Penguin Books, 2004); Tom Mertes, ed., *A Movement of Movements* (New York: Verso, 2004).

103 Apart perhaps from the interesting but quite specific experience of Quebec Solidaire: see Roger Rashi, "Quebec Solidaire: A Left of the Left Formation?" *The Bullet,* no. 286, December 11, 2009; Richard Fidler, "Quebec Left Debates Independence Strategy," *The Bullet,* no. 284, December, 7, 2009. We are leaving Mexico, with its many particularities, to the side in considering the North American Left but see: Richard Roman and Edur Velasco Arregui, "The Murder of a Union and the Rebirth of Class Struggle, Parts 1 and 2," *The Bullet,* November 25 and 26, 2009; Hepzibah Munoz-Martinez, "Crisis, Populist Neoliberalism and the Limits to Democracy in Mexico," *The Bullet,* December 15, 2009.

104 Stanley Aronowitz, *Left Turn: Forging a New Political Future* (Boulder: Paradigm, 2006); Greg Albo, "Neoliberalism and the Discontented," in *Socialist Register: Global Flashpoints: Reactions to Imperialism and Neoliberalism*, eds. Leo Panitch and Colin Leys (London: Merlin Press, 2008).

105 Marta Harnecker, *Rebuilding the Left* (London: Zed Books, 2007), 99. See also: Leo Panitch, *Renewing Socialism* (London: Merlin, 2008).

106 The foremost advocate of this position is the American bioregionalist Kirkpatrick Sale, *Human Scale* (New York: Coward, McCann & Geoghegan, 1980).

107 See Greg Albo, "The Limits of Eco-Localism: Scale, Strategy, Socialism," in *Coming to Terms with Nature, Socialist Register 200*, eds. L. Panitch and C. Leys (New York: Monthly Review, 2006).

108 Hilary Wainwright, *Arguments for a New Left: Answering the Free-Market Right* (Oxford: Blackwell, 1994), 264.